THE COLOUR COMPASS BOOK

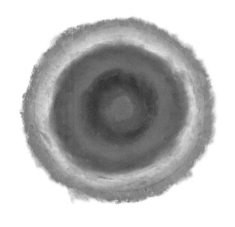

THE COLOUR COMPASS BOOK

Discover Your Personal Colours and Transform Your Life

Mary Lambert

CICO BOOKS

London

First published in Great Britain by Cico Books, 32 Great Sutton Street, London EC1V 0NB

Copyright © Cico Books 2001, Text copyright © Mary Lambert 2001

10 9 8 7 6 5 4 3 2 1
ISBN 1 903116 38 4
A CIP catalogue record for this book is available from the British Library
Managing Editor: Georgina Harris; Editor: Mandy Greenfield; Design: Ian Midson; Illustrations: Lucy Bristow

Printed and bound in Singapore by Tien Wah Press

Author's acknowledgments

I would like to thank Cindy Richards for supporting this book idea, and Georgina Harris for her hard work in project managing this book in such a short space of time. Also Ian Midson for his innovative design and Lucy Bristow for her beautiful artworks. Finally, as ever, many thanks to my family and all my friends, my cats Rama and Zita, for supporting and encouraging me during the ups and downs of writing.

Further reading:
Colour therapy, Pauline Wills, Element
Colour your life, H & D Sun, Piatkus
Colour healing, Pauline Wills, Piatkus
Colour healing, A Walters & G Thompson, Thorsons
Complete book of colour, Suzy Chiazzari, Element
Feng shui for modern living, Stephen Skinner & Mary Lambert, Cima Books
Essential feng shui, Simon Brown, Ward Lock
Lillian Too's Easy-to-use feng shui – 168 ways to success, Collins & Brown

Mary Lambert is based in London, UK, and can be contacted for feng shui consultations on homes and businesses and for clutter clearing sessions on 0800 975 6021.

Contents

Introduction

Color denotes our personalities, dreams, and desires. It can drain energy or inspire vitality, helping or hindering attitudes and emotions. Every day is punctuated with color choices, yet this is so instinctive that this craving for color goes virtually unnoticed. Whether you choose the black pen or the blue, or decide between that luscious scarlet strawberry mousse and a 'good' green apple, subconsciously a personal color code is guiding you, which helps you express deeper emotional and physical needs. In this book you will find many practical ways to use color to help balance your emotions, create a focus for your goals, heal physical ailments, and bring harmony into your home.

Parts One and Two of this book reveal how you can empower your life through selecting the right colors to wear, boosting your mood and wellbeing through food and color, and how you can benefit from the color healing used in many complementary therapies. It also explains the scientific impact of color on the mind and body. Part Three shows how to use color in the home, with ancient feng shui principles and the Five Element system so that you can improve key areas of your life, from health to love and wealth. Both 'inner' and 'external' colors are considered because our outer reality is often indicative of our inner, or emotional, discomfort. As you work through this book, consider that color is one of the most effective messengers we have between our subliminal feelings and rational, conscious mind. With this understanding, you can use color to make real changes that will affect you immediately.

The colors within you

Every day, we make choices based on color. We select clothes of a color that reflects the needs of the day ahead: vibrant red for a busy meeting, or calming blues for dealing with difficult people. Next time you select food of a particular color, think about what important needs you are satisfying other than your hunger. Yellow foods, for example, such as bananas, are thought to give mental stimulation, while green foods are considered calming, and to help to balance emotions. A plateful of foods of mixed colors provides the best blend of color energies which will help to keep the body healthy. It is a scientifically proven fact that eating a multicolored diet is good for you.

Not surprisingly, color is regularly used in a number of complementary therapies, such as reiki, to strengthen the healing energy. These therapies will also bring about a heightened awareness in you that the body and the spiritual centers speak their mind with color. The more you use color, the more you will become aware of your varying moods and your body's need for energy, serenity, or healing. Ignoring your body's messages can stop you from feeling 'at one' with your inner and outer self so that more serious imbalances in energy and ailments may occur.

You can also treat yourself to some simple but effective color treatments at home. Color meditation exercises can bring you calm and peace, restoring balance to the body and spirit.

The colors within your home

Your home is your personal sanctuary from the stresses and strains of the world. It is here that you relax and spend time with those you love in the ways you wish. Time spent at home is invaluable for rebalancing your energies. In the light of this, it is extremely important that you use the powerful effects of color to your advantage.

Choosing the right hues and tones for your home, based on its direction and the Five Element system, creates a positive space and is also a lot of fun. Large areas of color, such as that on walls and floors, have a profound effect on your physical, mental, and spiritual wellbeing, whether you want to create a peaceful haven in which to relax, or an energizing room for socializing. Small, inexpensive accessories or decorative touches are ideal for introducing the right calming or energizing color when and where you need it.

With this book, you will learn to decipher your own color code and discover a new palette of tones and hues that will bring you more energy, success, and balance, and ultimately provide an almost magical formula for living well. Read on to find out how.

How color affects us

CONTENTS

Color permeates the world, and all cultures are influenced by it. We see it all around us in nature – in the blue of the sky, the yellow of the sun, the green of the grass. We take in color from the rays of the sun, absorbing the entire spectrum of colors through our eyes, our breath, and our skin. The colors' health-giving vibrations help our bodies to function normally. Color also works deep inside us, on our mind and emotions, changing the balance of our moods and our feelings of wellbeing – even our spiritual psyche.

In ancient cultures throughout the world, color also played an important role. Prehistoric people painted crude pictures on cave walls using elemental earth colors, while the early Egyptians used a basic palette on their tomb paintings. In religion, too, color is often strongly symbolic. Christians get married in white as a sign of purity, whereas in China red is the lucky color for marriage.

This section introduces the basics of color – its historical beginnings and its uses in religion, as well as the way in which its energizing vibrations give focus to our lives.

The origins and symbolism of color

Scenes of daily life were depicted by the ancient Egyptians in primary colors on papyrus, a type of paper that was made from reeds.

From ancient times color and light have been important to human existence. Despite having poor color vision, prehistoric people realized the importance of color, and early cave art was crudely hand-painted using natural pigments from the cave floor – red and yellow ocher, black manganese, and mud. Sometimes crystals in the cave walls introduced white into the paintings.

Symbolic hieroglyphics and imagery, and a limited color palette, were also employed in the descriptive tomb paintings of ancient Egypt dating from 3,000 B.C. In the Middle Ages, from about the fifth century A.D. to the start of the Renaissance in the fourteenth century, color use became more sophisticated and was displayed in castles, churches, and palaces. Pigment colors were now made by colorists, who supervised the grinding and blending of the different colors.

During the seventeenth century, the flamboyant Baroque style with its elaborate ornamentation took over, while in Victorian times the most significant color development was the use of aniline dyes, made from coal tar. These were first used in fabrics, and then in wallpaper and paint. In the late nineteenth century, the Arts and Crafts movement brought in a simpler palette of colors, such as ivory, pale gray, and olive green.

The oil- and water-based paints that we use today include a vast range of colors made with artificial dyes. More traditional ranges, based on Victorian or heritage colors, have also become popular in Britain as more people have set about restoring and renovating their Victorian and Edwardian homes.

Color for healing

Color was used as an early form of healing therapy. In ancient Atlantis, the lost civilization that sank beneath the sea, physical and mental illness were supposedly treated with color from crystals. And in ancient Greece, Hippocrates, known as the "father of medicine," gave early homeopathic treatments using colored dressings and ointments.

The symbolism of color

Numerous different cultures and religions throughout history have given colors special symbolic and religious significance in ceremonies, spirituality, and mysticism.

RED AND ORANGE
• This was symbolic of the ancient Egyptian sun god, Ra.
• Buddhism regards red as the color of creativity and life.
• In Japan and China, orange is the color of love and happiness. The Chinese represent this by the "fingered citron," a blessed fruit that resembles the hand of Buddha.

YELLOW
• For Hindus, bright yellow represents light, truth, and immortality; for Buddhists it is a sacred color – their monks wear saffron robes.
• For Christians, yellow implies something that is sacred and divine.

For the Chinese, red is the color of passion and luck, and represents the sun and the phoenix; the red phoenix is believed to represent opportunity, luck, strength, and immortality.

GREEN
• This is the color of growth/rebirth in European and Chinese tradition.
• In Islam, green is a sacred color, because Allah is never depicted as a personified being but is believed to be present in nature.

BLUE AND PURPLE
• In Christianity, the Virgin Mary is always shown wearing blue.
• For Buddhists, blue represents the calm of the heavens and waters.
• Purple is traditionally worn by priests for ceremonies, and by royalty .
• In Christianity, purple is the color of God, and is used during Lent.

WHITE AND BLACK
• In the West a white wedding gown stands for innocence and purity.
• In ancient Egypt, black was linked to deities and black cats were sacred.

What is color?

Color is a form of light, of electromagnetic radiation – energy that vibrates in the same way as heat, sound, and radio waves. It comes from the pure white light of sunlight, which is essential to enable our bodies to function healthily – mentally, physically, and spiritually. Getting enough sunlight can be a problem nowadays, because we spend so much time indoors, either working or traveling in enclosed cars or trains. The intrinsic color vibrations that come from the rays of sunlight all have special healing qualities that our bodies need.

We can see the colors in sunlight by passing them through a prism, which refracts the light and splits it up into the different frequencies of the eight colors of red, orange, yellow, green, turquoise, indigo, violet, and magenta (see page 15).

Every living thing or object comprises energy – modern physics has even accepted that solid objects are made of energy that simply vibrates at a different, "heavier" frequency. It is believed that color vibrates at a higher frequency than sound and therefore has a stronger effect on the human body, setting off more powerful chemical reactions. So all those popular phrases that we use – such as "red with anger," "green with envy," "feeling blue," and "in the pink" – are actually accurate descriptions of changes taking place in our electromagnetic field or our aura (see pages 56–57).

The electromagnetic spectrum

The radiation of color forms part of the electromagnetic spectrum. This spectrum starts with radio waves, which have a low frequency and long wavelengths, and works through infrared rays, visible light (containing the colors of the spectrum), and ultraviolet light, with each wavelength becoming shorter and the frequency higher. Cosmic rays, about which very little is known, have the shortest wavelength of all and the highest frequency. None of the frequencies, apart from the visible rays, can be seen by the human eye.

The different wavelengths

The qualities of all vibrating energies and the effects they produce are defined by two criteria. The first is wavelength: the actual distance between the vibrational waves as they emit from their source (which, in the case of visible light, is the sun). The second is the frequency of vibration: how many waves pass a certain point during a period of time (say, one minute). White or natural light contains a mixture of wavelengths and frequencies, while colored light always has a fixed wavelength and frequency. Red – a warm and stimulating electromagnetic energy – has the longest wavelength that we can see and the slowest vibrational frequency. Violet and the eighth color, magenta, on the other hand, are cool and calming energies, with the shortest wavelengths but the fastest vibrations.

The eight colors of the spectrum are needed for physical, mental, and spiritual wellbeing. We take in the colors through light impulses from the sun's rays.

13

How we sense color

The way that our bodies perceive color is through the light that enters our eyes. We also take in some light through our skin and the air that we breathe. We may often be subconsciously aware of the different color energies on our skins when some clothes seem to irritate us, while others feel comfortable and make us feel good.

How eyes interpret color

When light rays, made up of radiation of different wavelengths, enter our eyes, they pass through the pupil and the watery fluid (the aqueous humor) that protects it until they reach the lens. The eye lens – similar to a camera lens – bends or refracts these rays so that they focus on the retina, a thin light-sensitive tissue lining the back of the eye. When light hits the retina, it is changed into the nerve energy that allows us to see. The retina contains two types of cells – rods and cones – that have light-sensitive pigments.

The function of rods and cones

The rods are more sensitive to light, and allow us to see in dimly lit conditions or at night, but they cannot distinguish color. The cones are used in bright light and for color vision. There are three types of cones, each of which reacts to one of the three main spectrum colors. One type reacts to the long wavelengths of red-orange light; the second to the short wavelengths of green light; and the third to the shortest wavelengths of blue/violet (and magenta) light.

When light hits the retina, it causes a structural change in the pigment within a cone, making the cone release an electrical impulse that moves along the optic nerve to the visual areas (visual cortex) that are situated at the back of the brain. The cones seem to react better to certain light wavelengths than to others, but they respond

uniquely to each one. This explains to a certain extent how the retina recognizes different wavelengths, but it also seems to contain other cells that analyze the signals coming from the cones before they are sent to the brain, where further processing occurs. This allows for the final perception of color as we know it.

The eye can perceive millions of different hues, but if a group of color-receptive cones is missing from the retina, then we cannot define certain colors and are called "color-blind." This is an inherited condition that affects more men than women – and the most common problem is distinguishing between red and green colors.

When sunlight passes through a prism, it is refracted into the spectrum colors of red, orange, yellow, green, turquoise, indigo, violet, and magenta.

The vibrations of color

Blue is traditionally seen as a soothing color that is useful for promoting healing and a sense of calm.

The light impulses that we receive through our eyes are not only used for sight, but also affect the pituitary and pineal glands, which control different bodily and mental functions. The colored rays are also a living energy that influence our spiritual energy field, the aura (see pages 56–57). When energy blocks appear in this field, which includes all the colors of the spectrum, they can be the precursor of illness and may benefit from being treated with the color that relates to the chakra, the spiritual energy center (see pages 50–53) that is malfunctioning. Color healing (see pages 46–81) and other color therapies can bring about a dramatic response from a body that is ailing, either emotionally or physically.

Each color also has its own spectrum, ranging from very pale to a dark shade. Paler colors are produced with the addition of white, while darker shades have some black added. Colors also have both negative and positive attributes. Someone who has a clear, bright blue in their aura, for example, is displaying good health, whereas a murky, muddy blue indicates that there may be an inner disturbance.

Color and the emotions

Although we all react to the energy of different colors, each color also evokes a unique emotional response in us. So if ten people

looked at the color green, they would all respond differently, and a few might have a pleasant or unpleasant memory associated with that color, which would recur for years afterward. Some people might remember having a favorite green toy. Others might recall the unhappiness of being criticized by a teacher who often worn green.

Generally, we also respond more positively to the stronger energy of brighter, more vibrant colors, while looking at drabber, duller colors tends to depress us.

Orange is a warm, stimulating color which has been associated with love and happiness for thousands of years in the spiritual disciplines of the Far East.

Color in rooms

Everyone reacts individually to the vibrational energy of color that is on the walls of a room. So we may walk into a room and immediately feel relaxed and at peace; this will often happen in a blue room, because this color sends out calming, short energy-waves. In an orange room, however, the warmth and vibrancy of this color's longer wavelengths may make us feel refreshed and revitalized.

In feng shui – the ancient practice of good energy flow – bringing the right color vibrations into a house can create harmony and balance in it. By using the Five Element system, whereby you work out the orientation of each room (see pages 84–87), you can enhance the energy that is inherent in each room by painting it the color of its corresponding element. So if, for instance, your bedroom is the Wood element in the east, painting it a shade of green will create the right ambience and atmosphere.

Color associations

All colors have special attributes and general properties that create a reaction within us. Knowing the overall benefits of the different colors can help you use them to maximum benefit.

RED
Red is a vibrant, stimulating color at the hot end of the spectrum. Associated with ambition and new beginnings, it brings warmth and excitement and increases blood flow in the body. Persistence, physical drive, and power are all qualities of red. Too much red can induce anger or aggressive male energy, but is also "grounding."

ORANGE
Orange has some of the assertiveness of red, but is associated with more feminine, caring energies. It can bring good health, joy, and bliss, and reduce depression. Too much can, however, generate pride.

YELLOW
Yellow is the color of the sun, a stimulating hue associated with self-expression, logic, and intellectual abilities. It can bring hope and inspiration. Conversely, dull shades are linked to a negative attitude.

GREEN
Green is the color of nature, balance, and empathy for others. It soothes the emotions, calms stress, and gives security and protection. On the more stimulating side, green promotes decision-making skills. Negatively, a muddy shade can represent decay or death.

TURQUOISE
Turquoise is a cool, relaxing color that promotes wellbeing and soothes mental fatigue. It creates the opportunity for change. However, the dirtier shades can create an inability to progress in life.

BLUE

Blue is a very calm, cool color that can engender feelings of tranquility. A strong blue can develop your intuitive abilities, but too much can promote lethargy.

INDIGO, VIOLET, AND PURPLE

Indigo, made from blue and violet, is inspirational, and can increase imaginative ideas. A desire for indigo may reveal a need for mental space. Muddier shades can attract isolation and depression. Violet is a strong psychic color that boosts your intuition and imagination, while purple can induce calm and protects the psyche. The darker shades of both can, however, arouse manipulative tendencies.

MAGENTA (PINK)

Magenta is gentle, nurturing, and soothing. It projects compassion and unconditional and spiritual love. It may be too calming if you are feeling depressed.

WHITE

This is the color of purity and innocence. It offers protection, tranquility, and comfort, and can give you time for reflection. Being exposed to too much white can make you feel cold or isolated.

Red is a warm, energizing color and we often choose it when we want extra zest or stimulation in our lives.

GOLD AND SILVER

Gold is associated with abundance, higher wisdom, and understanding. It can reduce your fears and help counter a lack of interest in life. Silver relates to the color of the moon. It can encourage change, movement, and learning. It is a balancing and harmonizing color.

BLACK AND GRAY

Often seen as sophisticated, black may be protective, but is also mysterious. It is a passive color that can stop you moving on in life. Gray is a tranquil color, but is sometimes known as the color of noncommitment, and can prompt self-criticism.

BROWN

Brown is the color of the earth – a stable, grounding color. It encourages commitment, but murkier shades can weaken self-esteem.

Energize your life with color

CONTENTS

Color has such a strong influence on our lives that we are drawn to it almost magnetically. Subconsciously, our bodies need different colors and instinctively seem to know which ones we need to thrive. The different vibrations of each color even affect our moods, and change others' opinions of us in both negative and positive ways.

We can learn which colors make the most of us as individuals, and work toward renewed energy in all areas of our lives. The latest developments in color psychology, the best stimulating hues and calming shades, the right clothes to wear for the right occasion, and even the best colored foods to eat, are all valuable methods for changing the way we feel and live our lives.

This section discusses how color can increase our vitality on all levels, bringing contentment and fulfillment into everything we do.

Stimulating colors

In all areas of your life, color power can work for you. The force of every single shade and hue of each color of the spectrum has been scientifically examined; our eyes and skin constantly absorb the different vibrations of each color tint and transfer its information to our brains. The results are so powerful that color therapy is now in use worldwide in treating many physical ailments. More potently, we can harness the immediate effects of color in our daily lives simply by making the right color choices in the clothes we wear and the foods we eat.

In the US in the 1930s, Hindu scientist Dinshah P. Ghadiali pioneered color therapy. He researched the control that color vibrations have on all living organisms, including humans. His experiments revealed that specific colors enhanced the functioning of different organs, which led to the discovery that exposure to a certain color could benefit an ailing organ. He concluded that the human aura (the body's spiritual energy field) was integral to this process, because it absorbed the spectrum colors through sunlight, which energized parts of the body.

The power of color

Many people use color therapeutically when they are undergoing some life or emotional changes. If they have experienced a broken relationship, for example, they can find themselves drawn to wearing a shade of green, the color of the heart chakra. The energy gives them the boost they need to recover and move on.

When your life is changing dramatically, you may seek out the color that will give you extra momentum. If you are having problems banishing negative thoughts, you may be drawn to shades of peach, apricot, or orange, since this relates to the sacral chakra (see page 51) – spiritual area of creativity, happiness, and zest for life.

Find your own colors

The main colors that affect us are the rainbow hues of the color spectrum – red, orange, yellow, green, turquoise, indigo, purple, and magenta. If you feel you lack energy, experiment to find the particular color energy you need to improve your mental state or your health. Sitting quietly in a peaceful room, study the colored squares on this page, or make your own by drawing up all the colors on large card squares with colored pens. Now spend a few quiet minutes looking at each of the colors until you feel yourself being drawn to one color in particular. Your instinctive choice will be correct: continue to focus steadily on just this color, as it is this hue that your body and your emotions are seeking. As you focus, allow your mind and body to relax. It may take as long as 30 minutes to draw in enough of the color's stimulating energy. When you start to feel restless, this means that you have absorbed enough color, and it is time to stop.

Tip

Use the pendulum to ask any question about wellbeing in your daily life. Use it to find the different colors you need to relax, to help you sleep, or to energize you for a meeting.

Dowsing for color

Dowsing is an ancient practice that is used to find water, minerals, and oil. It can also detect blockages in the chakras (see pages 50–53), or ease health problems. Dowsing is an effective way of releasing subconscious energies; you can find the color that your body or your emotions need by dowsing for it. This is an intuitive way of choosing colors, as you bypass your conscious mind and ego and connect directly to your inner self. To dowse effectively, you need a pendulum to conduct your inner energies. You can either buy a pendulum with a natural quartz crystal (a powerful conductor of energy) or make one yourself. All you need is a chain or a piece of thin cord or string about 6 in (15cm) long, from which you hang a small weighted object, such as a raw crystal, a bead, or part of a glass necklace. Some dowsers have a natural affinity with their pendulum, but everyone can benefit from even the basic principles and use their pendulum to answer specific questions.

Checking the swing of the pendulum

Before you start working with colors, check the "yes" or "no" response from your pendulum. Hold the cord or chain loosely between your fingers and say to yourself, silently or out loud, the words, "Tell me what is yes." The pendulum should respond by swinging in a clockwise or counterclockwise direction. Note in which direction it swings, then ask which is the "no" direction. This will normally be the opposite of "yes." Also ask for the response for "don't know," which will often be a swinging motion from side to side. Commit these directions to memory, or write them down.

Finding your energy color

To find the color your body is lacking, either make up your own large color wheel (coloring it with paints or pens) following the one shown opposite, or dowse directly over this one.

Hold in your mind the question "Which color do I need today?" Hang the pendulum over each color and ask, "Do I need green?"or "Do I need yellow?" and so on as you go through the color spectrum

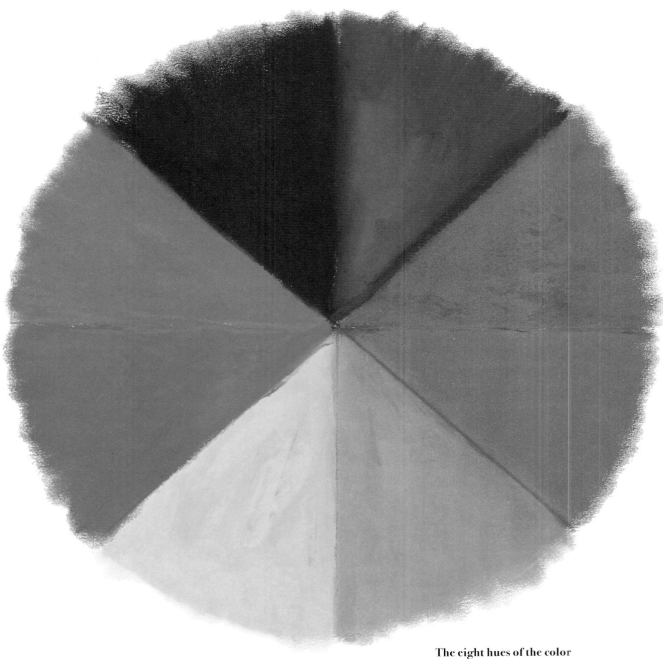

The eight hues of the color spectrum are often represented as a color wheel, so that opposite, or complementary, colors can easily be identified.

until you get a "yes" response. You will probably get a positive response from just one color, although it might be two if your chakras are out of balance. You can then ask whether you need a lighter or darker shade of "your" color. Now make up a card of that particular shade and place it by your desk, in your bag or briefcase, and look at it regularly so that you can absorb its healing vibrations.

Color and our moods

The colors to which we are naturally drawn are often reflected in the accessories and furnishings of our homes.

When you get up in the morning, what lies behind your decision to pick a specific outfit to wear that day? Your choice will (usually) be expressed through the color of your clothes, but why do you choose that particular color, and why do you sometimes wear a different color every day of the week?

We all have our favorite colors, which we like to include in the clothes we wear and in the furnishings and accessories of our home. However, the advantages of these colors go beyond the simple visual pleasures of an attractive image and a pleasant home; we can learn more about ourselves by studying our favorite colors, and we can find out how colors that we may not previously have thought of can give us more energy to make changes in our lives. Remember that if, in the morning, you have a problem choosing what to wear, it may mean that you have not yet found the color you need.

A rainbow of colors

Our bodies need the vibrational energy of all the colors contained in the rainbow to keep our chakras (our spiritual energy centers) and our organs balanced and healthy. If you have an imbalance in one color, then another color may become dominant and bring about upheaval. If you do not listen to the color messages that your body is sending you, and simply surround yourself with fashionable colors, then your internal color harmony may become disrupted.

The colors that you choose also mirror your current emotions, so if you are feeling negative, you may be drawn to wearing dull or dark colors such as black, gray, or brown. When you are stressed, you may find yourself regularly in neutral colors that won't put you under pressure.

Our bodies also dictate the energy we need, so if you suddenly feel the urge to buy a bright yellow shirt, it shows that you need an energy boost and some extra stimulation.

A change of life direction

Always listen to what your body tells you with regard to color, because it may be important. If you are seeking promotion at work, for instance, you may find yourself wanting to wear warmer, more vibrant colors, such as yellow and red, to match the creativity and expansion that you desire in your job. Conversely, if you have left a high-pressured corporate job in order to work in a more healing, relaxed environment as, say, an alternative-health therapist, then you may find yourself suddenly wearing more shades of green, as this is a peaceful, stable, and balancing color, and represents an ideal choice for the caring professions.

The desire to wear bright yellow may indicate a need for extra energy, but is also a sign of optimism.

All colors can work for you

It is interesting to analyze why we dislike some colors in particular. Sometimes the color in question is linked to bad emotional memories with a person or an event from our past. However, we really need energy from all the different colors, so, if you can't bear blue because it links in some way to a past failure, try wearing a very pale shade occasionally to reap some of its benefits. Given enough time, you may even begin to like the color.

Color and clothes

Clothes are a personal way of expressing our true selves through the colors that we choose to wear. Although the fashion industry offers us new shades for each season, we also need to understand the psychology behind color and learn to follow our internal color-health system to keep our bodies well and our emotions stable. The clothes we wear can act as color filters, determining how much color and light energy are absorbed by our physical body and our spiritual, or etheric, body – the aura.

When you are next out shopping, or on the way to work, look at what other people are wearing and note what it reveals about them. Someone who is wearing a pink top, for example, may be expressing love and compassion, while a brown suit may be a sign of a hard worker who is greatly attached to family and friends.

Clothes for work

The clothes that we wear to work may be very different from the ones that we wear at home or when out relaxing with friends. In the work environment, we need to project a professional image to gain respect and credibility from our bosses and colleagues.

Wearing a suit to work is often the accepted dress code for both men and women. Black or charcoal gray is often worn as a power symbol. If you go into a meeting wearing black, you are telling everybody that you have strong opinions and are a force to be reckoned with. When red is added, it creates more energy and dynamism, while yellow promotes positive mental stimulation, and blue is associated with improving your communication skills. But black also has negative connotations and can bring out your dark or depressive side, so someone with a shy or introverted personality could try wearing more nurturing brown to garner feelings of strength and security, rather than risk harsher head-to-toe black.

Color psychology

The colors of the clothes that you regularly wear show different aspects of your personality.

COLOR		WHAT YOU ARE TRYING TO PROJECT
	Red	A strong, passionate person who likes action and drama
	Orange	A courageous person who shows enthusiasm in everything they do
	Yellow	An intellectual person who likes being in control and in a position as a leader
	Green	A conventional person who prefers a balanced, secure life and appreciates nature
	Turquoise	An approachable person who communicates well and has a zest for life
	Blue	An honest, loyal person who wants a peaceful life
	Indigo/ violet/ purple	A distinguished person who is aware of their own self-worth and often works in a creative field
	Magenta	A person who is sensual and can easily show feelings of love and compassion
	Black	A person who is respectable and likes tradition, but can hide their inner feelings
	Gray	A self-reliant, independent person, but one who may be self-critical
	White	A self-protecting person or someone who has a rather detached personality
	Brown	A stable, secure person who is dedicated to friends and family

If you regularly have to give talks or host workshops, wearing red will energize you and keep your audience interested.

Dark blue in the workplace denotes confidence and a discerning and intuitive attitude to work. Neutral colors, such as tan or beige, are considered the best colors for team workers who share tasks regularly with their colleagues.

For those who take part frequently in public speaking, a duller neutral color will simply make them fade into the background, but a bright color, such as red or maroon, will help to catch the audience's attention.

Clothes for relaxation

When you meet work colleagues in social situations or over the weekend, you can often be surprised by how different they look away from the work situation where you are used to seeing them. In your weekend or evening clothes, you can truly express yourself, so this is the time to introduce some real color into your life.

Soft pastel colors bring you tranquility, helping you relax and unwind from the pressures of the week. Blues and greens are ideal for promoting a calming evening feeling, while white can bring peace and give you comfort. Violet and purple will reduce any upset, anxiety, or fears that you may have, and bring a sense of spiritual contentment.

If you are going out for the evening, the warmer, brighter colors of orange or red will inspire conversation and sociability, leading to lively conversation over the dinner table. Black may be a favorite evening color for many people, but don't wear it when you are really stressed, because it may make you feel more introverted than you usually feel, and it can also reinforce dark moods. Those who prefer dark shades for evening should also avoid deep blue, which can be depressing, and purple, which can bring out negative, manipulative tendencies.

Clothes that boost your health

The different fabrics that we wear act as light and color filters, so that when natural light passes through them, it transmits the necessary color vibration to our bodies.

We need all the colors of the spectrum for optimum health. The extra colors of black, gray, white, and brown also affect our moods. Some fabric colors, such as white, allow all the light vibrations to pass through, so that we take in balanced amounts of them; this has a cleansing effect on the body and makes us feel good. Black fabric, on the other hand, reflects light, which is why it is often viewed negatively. Be careful of wearing too much black, because the lack of light energy reaching your body can affect your health detrimentally. You may also be denying the "light" inside yourself.

As the energy from different colors influences us so strongly, when we are not feeling well or functioning at our peak we can choose the color of clothes that our body actually needs. In this way, color can help to fix a health problem before it becomes an illness.

When you are not able to wear clothes of the color you feel your body requires, you can accessorize instead. Scarves, bags, or jewelry of the right color can bring in the necessary energies.

Accessorizing

It is not always possible to wear the color that you feel you need, either because there is a regulation dress code that you have to follow, or because you are required to wear a uniform at work. However, you can bring in the color of your choice by clever accessorizing: by choosing jewelry with colored stones, by adding scarves, gloves, or bags to your outdoor wear. You can simply carry a crystal of the relevant color in your pocket for its healing properties (see pages 66–69) and the necessary colored energies.

How the colors of our clothes affect our health

COLOR		POSITIVE ASSOCIATION	NEGATIVE ASSOCIATION
	Red	Stimulates vitality and energy, helps when we feel tired and down; aids anemia and colds	Avoid if you are angry, or have high blood pressure or conditions such as flu or CFS (Chronic Fatigue Syndrome)
	Magenta (and pink)	Boosts the nervous system, relieves headaches and colds, and improves the functioning of the heart	Can fuel a lack of self-love, and bring on feelings of insecurity and isolation
	Orange	Helps creativity; boosts the nervous and respiratory systems, and can relieve the pain of abdominal cramps	Not a good color if you feel frustrated or sad; aggravates feelings of nausea
	Yellow	Brings inspiration and good self-expression; beneficial for indigestion and inflammatory problems of the joints and body tissues	Can produce irritability and exhaustion; may cause further self-criticism
	Green	Soothes the emotions, and is good for general healing and restoring the body cells; aids heart and lung problems and dissolves blood clots	Can bring about stagnation, repression, and feelings of jealousy
	Turquoise blue/blue	Calms tension and induces life changes; reduces swellings, heals cuts and bruises, and soothes burns and headaches	Avoid if you are depressed; it is not stimulating and can increase feelings of isolation
	Purple/ violet	Encourages dignity and respect; helps to stabilize the hormones; can treat neuralgia and mental stresses	Avoid if you lack stamina or are feeling very sensitive
	White	Gives insight into life, and purifies the body on all levels; can alleviate pain	Can increase feelings of isolation; bad for making decisions
	Black	Helps to provide self-sufficiency, control, and protection	If you feel depressed or in self-denial, black can make you reject help from others

Foods for stimulation and balance

Red foods, including red apples, strawberries, tomatoes, and red bell peppers, are full of iron, which can help to increase stamina and vitality.

We can balance the color vibrations that our bodies require through the food that we eat. In the traditional healing systems of the East, it is acknowledged that each part of the body, which relates to a spiritual center known as a chakra, may be stimulated or calmed by one particular color. Every food is a specific color, and it will directly affect our energy levels by stimulating the organs it affects and the spiritual energies of the chakras.

You may find yourself attracted to a particular color of food. For stimulation, you will naturally be drawn to eat more red, orange, and yellow foods, but if you need calming or a more balanced energy, you may seek green or blue foods. When your brain needs nutrients, you might be drawn to darker-colored foods, such as purple and indigo.

So if you are feeling stressed, are suffering from a minor infection, have an ongoing physical weakness, or just want to stay healthy, choose whatever color of food you need to support your wellbeing. By experimenting with different colors in your diet, you can find out more about the nutritional needs of your body and listen to what it is saying to you. As well as relating to chakra colors, each color of food you eat will have a specific purpose. Red foods, for instance, are known to stimulate energy production, while blue foods promote calm. Green foods improve heart function.

Red foods for energy

(Root chakra: lower pelvic area and adrenal glands)

Strawberries, red cherries, red plums, red apples, watermelons, raspberries, redcurrants, rhubarb, radishes, beets, tomatoes, red bell peppers, red kidney beans, red lentils, red meat.

These red foods are rich in iron, so they are good for people who are not functioning well, lack stamina, or are suffering from anemia. They also help to raise energy levels, cleanse the blood, and contain high levels of potassium for extra vitality. It is worth noting that, although they are not red in color, leafy green vegetables contain red energy.

Special benefits

• Tomatoes contain the antioxidant vitamins E, C, beta-carotene, and lycopene (a carotene), which are believed to help fight the free radicals that can cause the formation of cancer cells.

• Raspberries, strawberries, and red apples are full of vitamin C.

• Red kidney beans are high in soluble fiber, which slows digestion and reduces cholesterol levels.

Orange foods for good digestion

(Sacral chakra: kidneys, bladder, intestines, and ovaries/gonads)

Oranges, satsumas, tangerines, apricots, mangoes, papaya, peaches, nectarines, orange bell peppers, pumpkins, carrots, egg yolks.

Orange foods are rich in enzymes that encourage a healthy appetite and aid digestion. They are full of vitamins that provide more energy, encourage a healthy sex drive, and help strengthen the immune system.

Special benefits

• Citrus fruits are high in the antioxidant vitamin C, contain pectin (which reduces blood cholesterol) and flavenoids (which strengthen the blood capillaries).

• Carrots contain the carotene antioxidants and are also high in both soluble fiber (which lowers blood cholesterol) and in the substance beta-carotene (which can help to protect the body against lung cancer).

Orange foods, which include Chinese gooseberries and carrots, can boost the appetite, while oranges help to lower blood cholesterol.

Yellow foods for cleansing

(Solar plexus chakra: spleen, stomach, liver, and pancreas)

Lemons, grapefruit, melons, bananas, pineapples, corn, nuts and seeds, yellow lentils, yellow bell peppers, butter, vegetable oils.

Yellow-colored foods help detoxify the body, particularly the liver, gall bladder, pancreas, and spleen. Because of the slightly acidic nature of many of these foods, they keep the digestive system working well. They also boost the nervous system and stimulate the brain.

Special benefits

• Bananas are a good source of potassium, which aids the removal of sodium, promoting blood flow; and of carbohydrates (which provide a balanced rise in energy).

• Corn can balance blood-sugar levels and is high in iron, low levels of which cause tiredness, and potassium.

Green foods for a strong heart

(Heart chakra: lower lungs, heart, and thymus gland)

Grapes, kiwi fruit, limes, green apples, broccoli, leafy green vegetables, lettuce, zucchini (courgettes), peas, avocado. Green foods bring about body harmony. Green is the color of balancing energy and is important in your daily diet. Green foods are a good source of soluble fiber, and their juices cleanse the blood of toxins and aid the function of the lymphatic system. They can regularize blood pressure and balance alkaline/acidic levels.

Special benefits

• Broccoli is high in the antioxidant vitamins C, E, and beta-carotene. It is also a rich source of folate and iron, which help to prevent anemia in pregnancy.

• Avocado is high in vitamin E, which is essential for healthy blood, tissue, and cells.

Blue and indigo foods to calm and nurture

(Throat chakra: upper lungs and throat, thyroid and parathyroid glands: Third eye chakra: brainstem, pituitary and pineal gland)

Blueberries, bilberries, blackcurrants, black grapes, damsons, black cherries, raisins, prunes, juniper berries, black soybeans, olives, some oily fish, such as salmon, mackerel, or tuna.

Blue and indigo foods are cooling and soothe the body. They aid sleep, reducing the frenzied activity that is characteristic of over-stimulated brains.

Special benefits

• Blackcurrants are high in antioxidant vitamins C, E, and carotenes and are also anti-inflammatory, so can help fight throat infections.

• Oily fish contains omega-3 fatty acids, which protect against heart disease and blood clots.

Left: Yellow foods aid digestion and keep the nervous system working well, so eat plenty of lemons, grapefruit, bananas, melon, and corn.

Left: Green foods, such as mangetout, apples, bell peppers, and grapes can help to remove toxins and bring balance to the body.

Violet foods for creative ideas

(Crown chakra: brain and pineal gland)

Blackberries, purple grapes, eggplant (aubergines), purple onions, cabbages, turnips, globe artichokes.

The energy of violet foods is needed by the pineal gland (situated at the base of the brain) to nourish spiritual and creative areas of the body. Eating more violet food can help to develop inner knowledge and intuition.

Special benefits

• Blackberries are a good low-fat source of vitamin E.

• Purple onions contain properties that help reduce cholesterol levels; they also combat infections such as colds, coughs, and flu.

Violet foods, including purple grapes, turnips, and blackberries, can help develop your creative side.

Feng shui and color

Feng shui, which literally means "wind" and "water," is the ancient art of energy flow in the home. It has been practiced successfully in Chinese homes for thousands of years.

It is now becoming increasingly popular in the West, as people find out that, by following its principles of furniture placement and the right use of color, they can dramatically improve the atmosphere in their homes, their relationships, and their lives, and thus increase their overall happiness and wellbeing.

Feng shui works on the basis that there are energy currents – known as chi – that flow through the home. When these flow freely, the home's atmosphere is vibrant and positive, but when blockages and other obstructions are present, the energy of the home can stagnate and may damage the health and attitudes of the people living there. Chi also flows through our bodies, and, when we experience blockages, illness or discomfort can occur. Treatments such as acupuncture, traditional Chinese medicine, and shiatsu work on these blockages to get energy flowing properly again, by stimulating points that are linked to meridians (energy channels) and the body's organs.

The tai chi symbol (top) shows the opposite forces of yin and yang in a state of balance. In the home, ceramic yang items can be balanced by soft yin furnishings.

The forces of yin and yang

The opposing forces of yin and yang energies are seen as a central part of feng shui. Yin is considered a female energy: dark, passive, representing the earth, darkness, the moon, and death, while yang is male: positive and bright and representing heaven, light, the sun, and life. The tai chi symbol graphically shows the interaction of yin and yang, and how one cannot exist without the other. Inside our bodies, and in the home, yin and yang must balance for good health. For instance, in a living room, you may create balance by blending hard, yang accessories such as a mirror or metal and ceramic ornaments, with softer, yin items, such as cushions, curtains, throws, and rugs.

The Five Elements and what they mean

In the chart below, "strong" elements require weaker shades of the relevant colors than "small" elements.

ELEMENT	LIFE ASPIRATION	DIRECTION/ SEASON	COLOR	SHAPE	TRIGRAM	
Fire	Recognition and fame	South/summer	Red	Triangular	Li	
Earth	Marriage and romantic happiness; education and knowledge	Southwest (strong Earth), northeast (small Earth)/ late summer	Yellow/beige	Square, horizontal	Ku'un	Ken
Metal	Children, mentors, and networking	West (small Metal), northwest (strong Metal)/ fall	White, silver, and gold	Dome-shaped, circular	Tui	Ch'ien
Water	Career prospects	North/winter	Blue, black	Wavy, irregular	K'an	
Wood	Wealth and prosperity	East (strong Wood), southeast (small Wood) /spring	Green	Upright	Chen	Sun

The Five Elements and their colors

When you have figured out the directions of your home by using a compass (see pages 84–86), you will find out which elements govern specific areas, as each element is linked to a direction (see page 39).

The Five Elements are Fire, Earth, Metal, Water, and Wood, and these are the core feng shui energies that are present everywhere. They are also linked to the Pa Kua, the eight-sided diagnostic tool that is essential to a feng shui consultant for mapping out a home. Each element on the Pa Kua is associated with a color, a trigram (a three-line symbol), and a life aspiration (see page 39); for example, Fire is red, has the trigram known as Li, and relates to the aspirational area of recognition and fame. It is by using the element colors in the correct areas of your home that you can make an immense difference to its overall appeal and ambience.

In the Five Element Cycle elements interact with each other. In the Productive Cycle, each element harmoniously feeds the others, i.e., Wood feeds Fire and Fire feeds Earth. In the Exhausting Cycle, each calms the other. In the Controlling or Destructive Cycle, Wood is controlled by Metal, and Water by Earth.

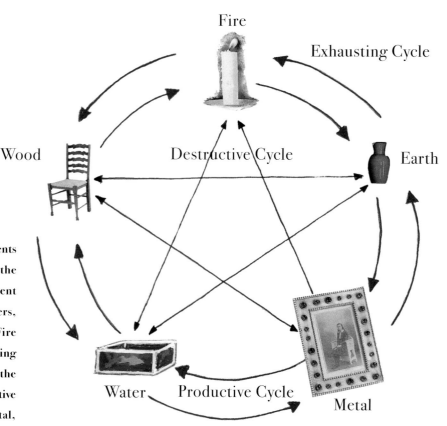

Using color as part of the interactive cycles

The elements are controlled by interactive cycles (see opposite). In the Productive (feeding) Cycle, each element produces another; for example, Wood produces Fire, Fire produces Earth, and so on around the circle. In the Destructive (controlling) Cycle, Fire is controlled by Water, Earth is controlled by Wood, etc. There is also an Exhausting (calming) Cycle that can be used. In this cycle, Metal calms Earth, Earth calms Fire, and so the process continues.

To create harmony in your home, you can use the vibrational energy of the element colors in your decorating schemes. This can have a powerful effect on you and your family, and encourage positive changes and progress. You can then use the interactive cycles to bring the color of a boosting or calming energy into a particular room, and be aware of its controlling energies. For instance, if you have an Earth room that faces southwest, you can enhance it by painting it yellow (the color of strong Earth). If you want to bring in a more uplifting energy, you can place a red throw or cushions on your sofa, because Fire produces Earth in the Element Cycle. You would want only a little green in the room, because Wood controls Earth in the Element Cycle, and only a dash of blue or black, because Water clashes with Earth. If in a bedroom you want slower, calmer energies to promote a good night's sleep, you could add some white via the quilt or bedspread, pillows, and sheets, because Metal calms Earth in the Element Cycle.

You can even use this Five Element system on yourself. For instance, increase your vitality by wearing clothes of the color of your birth element (see pages 42–45).

The different ways in which you can use feng shui color in your home are discussed in greater detail in Part 3. However, gaining a basic understanding of the way in which the elements interact will help you learn how to use them to positive effect in your home. This in turn will make your house work with you, so that it becomes a pleasant, stimulating environment that nurtures and inspires both you and your family.

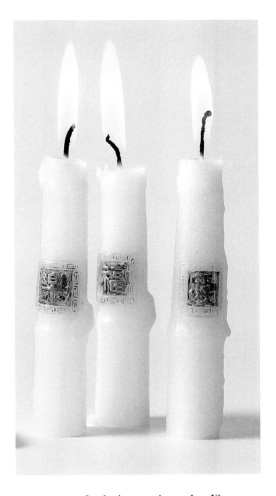

In the interactive cycles, Fire produces Earth, is controlled by Water, and calms Wood. The Fire element is associated with a very stimulating, positive energy.

Identifying your birth element and color

You can find the ideal color to wear, or the color that will give you a psychological boost, by using the Five Element system described on pages 40–41 – the stronger the color that you wear, the more positive you will feel. First, however, you need to find your feng shui birth date and element by using the Chinese lunar calendar (see opposite). You were born under one of the 12 astrological animals in the Chinese lunar calendar: the Ox, Tiger, Rabbit, Dragon, Snake, Horse, Sheep, Monkey, Rooster, Dog, Boar, or Rat, and have a corresponding birth and year element. The Chinese New Year starts on different days in January or February.

For instance, if you were born in February, 1960, you are a Rat animal influenced by the Water element (your year element is Metal), so the best color for you to wear is either blue or black. If you need an energy boost, wear some white with gold or silver jewelry, as Metal produces Water in the Element Cycle (see pages 40–41). Consider your year element as well. In this case, it is Metal, which is fine to wear since it is your boosting element. However, sometimes these elements will clash and, although a color may be a bad birth color, it may be a good color for your year element. Experiment and see how you feel while wearing the various colors that relate to you.

Also study the Productive and Destructive Cycles of the Five Elements, so that you can understand how the formula works. The chart on page 45 highlights your good colors, but also makes you aware of the colors that you may feel uncomfortable wearing, because they drain your energy. For example, for a Wood person, white (metal and gold) is not a favorable color, as Metal destroys Wood in the Element Cycle.

Birth-element chart

Discover what your family's birth elements are by using the chart below. And take note of your year element, which also influences the color of the clothes that you wear.

ANIMAL	BIRTH ELEMENT	BIRTH DATES	YEAR ELEMENT	ANIMAL	BIRTH ELEMENT	BIRTH DATES	YEAR ELEMENT
Ox	Earth	24 Jan. 1925–12 Feb. 1926	Wood	Dragon	Earth	13 Feb. 1964–1 Feb. 1965	Wood
Tiger	Wood	13 Feb. 1926–1 Feb. 1927	Fire	Snake	Fire	2 Feb. 1965–20 Jan. 1966	Wood
Rabbit	Wood	2 Feb. 1927–22 Jan. 1928	Fire	Horse	Fire	21 Jan. 1966–8 Feb. 1967	Fire
Dragon	Earth	23 Jan. 1928–9 Feb. 1929	Earth	Sheep	Earth	9 Feb. 1967–29 Jan. 1968	Fire
Snake	Fire	10 Feb. 1929–29 Jan. 1930	Earth	Monkey	Metal	30 Jan. 1968–16 Feb. 1969	Earth
Horse	Fire	30 Jan. 1930–16 Feb. 1931	Metal	Rooster	Metal	17 Feb. 1969–5 Feb. 1970	Earth
Sheep	Earth	17 Feb. 1931–5 Feb. 1932	Metal	Dog	Earth	6 Feb. 1970–26 Jan. 1971	Metal
Monkey	Metal	6 Feb. 1932–25 Jan. 1933	Water	Boar	Water	27 Jan. 1971–14 Feb. 1972	Metal
Rooster	Metal	26 Jan. 1933–13 Feb. 1934	Water	Rat	Water	15 Feb. 1972–2 Feb. 1973	Water
Dog	Earth	14 Feb. 1934–3 Feb. 1935	Wood	Ox	Earth	3 Feb. 1973–22 Jan. 1974	Water
Boar	Water	4 Feb. 1935–23 Jan. 1936	Wood	Tiger	Wood	23 Jan. 1974–10 Feb. 1975	Wood
Rat	Water	24 Jan. 1936–10 Feb. 1937	Fire	Rabbit	Wood	11 Feb. 1975–30 Jan. 1976	Wood
Ox	Earth	11 Feb. 1937–30 Jan. 1938	Fire	Dragon	Earth	31 Jan. 1976–17 Feb. 1977	Fire
Tiger	Wood	31 Jan. 1938–18 Feb. 1939	Earth	Snake	Fire	18 Feb. 1977–6 Feb. 1978	Fire
Rabbit	Wood	19 Feb. 1939–7 Feb. 1940	Earth	Horse	Fire	7 Feb. 1978–27 Jan. 1979	Earth
Dragon	Earth	8 Feb. 1940–26 Jan. 1941	Metal	Sheep	Earth	28 Jan. 1979–15 Feb. 1980	Earth
Snake	Fire	27 Jan. 1941–14 Feb. 1942	Metal	Monkey	Metal	16 Feb. 1980–4 Feb. 1981	Metal
Horse	Fire	15 Feb. 1942–4 Feb. 1943	Water	Rooster	Metal	5 Feb. 1981–24 Jan. 1982	Metal
Sheep	Earth	5 Feb. 1943–24 Jan. 1944	Water	Dog	Earth	25 Jan. 1982–12 Feb. 1983	Water
Monkey	Metal	25 Jan. 1944–12 Feb. 1945	Wood	Boar	Water	13 Feb. 1983–1 Feb. 1984	Water
Rooster	Metal	13 Feb. 1945–1 Feb. 1946	Wood	Rat	Water	2 Feb. 1984–19 Feb. 1985	Wood
Dog	Earth	2 Feb. 1946–21 Jan. 1947	Fire	Ox	Earth	20 Feb. 1985–8 Feb. 1986	Wood
Boar	Water	22 Jan. 1947–9 Feb. 1948	Fire	Tiger	Wood	9 Feb. 1986–28 Jan. 1987	Fire
Rat	Water	10 Feb. 1948–28 Jan. 1949	Earth	Rabbit	Wood	29 Jan. 1987–16 Feb. 1988	Fire
Ox	Earth	29 Jan. 1949–16 Feb. 1950	Earth	Dragon	Earth	17 Feb. 1988–5 Feb. 1989	Earth
Tiger	Wood	17 Feb. 1950–5 Feb. 1951	Metal	Snake	Fire	6 Feb. 1989–26 Jan. 1990	Earth
Rabbit	Wood	6 Feb. 1951–26 Jan. 1952	Metal	Horse	Fire	27 Jan. 1990–14 Feb. 1991	Metal
Dragon	Earth	27 Jan. 1952–13 Feb. 1953	Water	Sheep	Earth	15 Feb. 1991–3 Feb. 1992	Metal
Snake	Fire	14 Feb. 1953–2 Feb. 1954	Water	Monkey	Metal	4 Feb. 1992–22 Jan. 1993	Water
Horse	Fire	3 Feb. 1954–23 Jan. 1955	Wood	Rooster	Metal	23 Jan. 1993–9 Feb. 1994	Water
Sheep	Earth	24 Jan. 1955–11 Feb. 1956	Wood	Dog	Earth	10 Feb. 1994–30 Jan. 1995	Wood
Monkey	Metal	12 Feb. 1956–30 Jan. 1957	Fire	Boar	Water	31 Jan. 1995–18 Feb. 1996	Wood
Rooster	Metal	31 Jan. 1957–17 Feb. 1958	Fire	Rat	Water	19 Feb. 1996–6 Feb. 1997	Fire
Dog	Earth	18 Feb. 1958–7 Feb. 1959	Earth	Ox	Earth	7 Feb. 1997–27 Jan. 1998	Fire
Boar	Water	8 Feb. 1959–27 Jan. 1960	Earth	Tiger	Wood	28 Jan. 1998–15 Feb. 1999	Earth
Rat	Water	28 Jan. 1960–14 Feb. 1961	Metal	Rabbit	Wood	16 Feb. 1999–4 Feb. 2000	Earth
Ox	Earth	15 Feb. 1961–4 Feb. 1962	Metal	Dragon	Earth	5 Feb. 2000–23 Jan. 2001	Metal
Tiger	Wood	5 Feb. 1962–24 Jan. 1963	Water	Snake	Fire	24 Jan. 2001–11 Feb. 2002	Metal
Rabbit	Wood	25 Jan. 1963–12 Feb. 1964	Water	Horse	Fire	12 Feb. 2002–31 Jan. 2003	Water

Using the element shapes

You can bring the shapes of the elements into the patterns or cut of your clothing to enhance your best colors. If you discover from the birth-element chart that you are a Wood person and you wear a green shirt or skirt, then a striped pattern will further enhance it. If you wear an energizing blue or black dress for an important meeting, then a wavy pattern will lift the vibrational energy of this color; alternatively, choose a style with a wavy hem or collar. If you are an Earth element person, a yellow or beige jumper will make you feel good, and to emphasize this element further, a subtle checked pattern will strengthen the effect of the color on you. To get some more energy, you could wear a red scarf or skirt – this would make a great combination for an interview, when you are in need of some extra confidence.

An Earth person will feel at her best dressed in yellow or beige. This could be further emphasized by a checked or horizontally striped pattern or boosted by a little red.

Color for romance

If you are a woman and have an important date with someone you really like, wearing a red dress will ensure that you make the right impression, because red gives out yang, positive energy and can boost the chances of a successful romance. However, do not choose a shade that is too strong or it may be overpowering. A man can make himself more desirable to a new partner by wearing a red tie or a pink shirt to bring in some of the passionate Fire energy. However, avoid wearing red if your birth element is Water or Metal, because red clashes with these elements and will drain you.

The best colors for you

ELEMENT	COLOR	BOOSTING COLOR	NEGATIVE COLOR	ELEMENT SHAPE	MIXING SHAPE WITH COLORS
Fire	Red	Green/brown	Blue/black; also white, silver, and gold	Triangles, stars, zigzag patterns	Mixes well with: yellow/beige background. Good with: red background. Auspicious on: green/brown background.
Earth	Yellow/beige	Red	Green/brown; also blue/black	Checks, horizontal stripes, wide rectangles	Mixes well with: white background. Good with: yellow/beige background. Auspicious on: red background.
Metal	White (silver and gold)	Yellow/beige	Red; also green/brown	Round shapes, dots, circles, dome, and oval shapes	Mixes well with: blue/black background. Good with: white background (could have gold/silver dots on white). Auspicious on: yellow/beige background.
Water	Blue/black	White (silver and gold)	Yellow/beige; also red	Wavy shapes, cloud shapes	Mixes well with: green/brown background. Good with: yellow/beige background. Auspicious on: white background.
Wood	Green	Blue/black	White (metal and gold); also yellow/beige	Vertical stripes, tall thin stripes	Mixes well with: red background. Good with: green/brown background. Auspicious on: blue/black background.

Color healing

CONTENTS

Healing with color is not a new therapy, for it has been used in different forms throughout history and is believed to have been practiced by the ancient culture in Atlantis in a very powerful way. Illness is thought to start in our aura, the body's spiritual energy field, when emotional imbalances occur in the energy centers, known as the chakras. All the chakras are linked to a color, so when a blockage is found, treating a particular chakra with its color helps to bring about balance and healing. Existing physical illnesses can also benefit from treatment, as the body organs and glands are intrinsically linked to the chakras.

Color therapy, administered by a qualified healer, is the most popular treatment and has been clinically proven to help diseases such as asthma and high blood pressure. In crystal healing the colored energies of a crystal are chosen by a therapist to match the ailing chakra. You can learn simple meditations or breathing exercises to heal yourself and take in the color that your body is craving. Healing can even be invoked in your dreams. This section discusses the different healing techniques with colors to bring your body back to emotional, physical, and spiritual harmony.

Color and your body

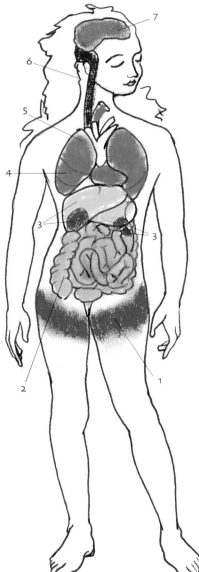

The seven glands of the endocrine system are linked to the body's organs and also correspond to the chakras.

Color is a powerful tool to use in physical healing, as all the organs and glands of the body react to the vibrations that come from different colors. For example, the kidneys react to the color orange, while the heart responds to green. When an area of the body is not working at full strength, its vibration will change and weaken. But, by wearing the color that links to this body part, or by being treated with it in a different way (such as with color therapy; see pages 58–61), the vibration can be restored to its normal, healthy level. So if your liver function is below par, yellow is the color to wear to give it a boost. Even drinking a banana milkshake will help.

The organs and the endocrine system

The body's organs and the endocrine system can be stimulated by the use of color (see opposite). In color therapy and other healing methods, the endocrine system – which consists of seven glands, headed by the pituitary gland – controls the body's hormones and the chakras (seven main spiritual energy centers, see pages 50–53), which are thought to be intrinsically linked with the position of the glands, corresponding to the seven main chakra points. So if an endocrine gland is stimulated by its associated color, then the chakra connected with it will also benefit. Conversely, if an endocrine gland is malfunctioning, our hormones will be out of balance, which will strongly affect our moods and also the spiritual energy of the chakra. If a chakra is not working well and the imbalance is not corrected, it will eventually manifest as a physical ailment in the body's organs and glands. So it is important to keep the endocrine glands working well with treatments such as color healing, because a hormonal imbalance is hard to correct, as hormones need to fall within a precise range of activity for good health.

The physical and the spiritual body

ORGAN/BODY PART	ENDOCRINE GLAND	COLOR		CHAKRA
Lower pelvic area (1)	Adrenals	Red		Root (1st)
Kidneys, bladder, large and small intestines (2)	Ovaries/gonads	Orange		Sacral (2nd)
Spleen, stomach, and liver (3)	Pancreas	Yellow		Solar plexus (3rd)
Lower lungs and heart (4)	Thymus	Green (rose)		Heart (4th)
Upper lungs and throat (5)	Thyroid and parathyroids	Turquoise blue		Throat (5th)
Brainstem (medulla oblongata) (6)	Pituitary and pineal	Indigo		Third eye (6th)
Brain (cerebral cortex) (7)	Pineal	Violet (white and gold)		Crown (7th)

(Note: the eighth spectrum color, magenta, is believed to link to the aura/spirit, and not to a chakra.)

Color and the chakras

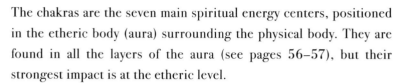

The chakras are the seven main spiritual energy centers, positioned in the etheric body (aura) surrounding the physical body. They are found in all the layers of the aura (see pages 56–57), but their strongest impact is at the etheric level.

Five of the chakras are situated along the spine, with the first being positioned at the base, the sixth located in the middle of the forehead, and the seventh on the crown of the head. The word chakra is an old Sanskrit term meaning "wheel," and psychics are said to see each chakra as a spinning wheel. Each one takes in energy from light that constantly moves and pulsates, and the wheels are believed by Indians to resemble the petals of the lotus flower, which open and close. They are emotional centers that relate to a specific color, emotional function, physical organ, or body part, and endocrine-gland function (see pages 48–49). The size of the chakras is thought to be linked to how much a person has developed spiritually. As already discussed, the chakras are believed to be directly associated with the endocrine system and are influenced by how well the glands are working, and vice versa. The body organs will also suffer the negative effects of the relevant malfunctioning chakra.

How the chakras react to color

The colors associated with each chakra correspond to the ones that affect the endocrine system and body organs (see opposite). Each chakra is sensitive to a light vibration or energy associated with the colors of the rainbow, which makes it resonate at a certain frequency. However, this energy – which moves through all the seven chakras in the body – can become blocked or disturbed because of an emotional upset or extreme stress. The body becomes unhealthy when this energy is not balanced or corrected, allowing toxins to accumulate; in time, physical illness can follow.

The chakras and the physical body

THE SEVEN CHAKRAS	EMOTIONAL FUNCTION	COLOR	ENDOCRINE GLAND/ BODY PART
Root chakra (1st) (bottom of spine)	Survival and self-preservation; blockages cause an inflexible or aggressive attitude to life	Red	Adrenal glands/ lower pelvic area
Sacral chakra (2nd) (pelvic area)	Controls creativity, security, and sexuality; blockages can inhibit physical closeness and cause frigidity	Orange	Ovaries and gonads/ kidneys, bladder, large and small intestines
Solar-plexus chakra (3rd) (upper abdomen below breastbone)	Connected to intellect, logic, personal achievement, and speaking boldly; blockages can bring mental problems	Yellow	Pancreas/stomach, spleen, and liver
Heart chakra (4th) (center of chest)	Our love center, which controls our relationships and feelings; blockages can make it hard to give or receive love	Green (rose)	Thymus/lower lungs and heart
Throat chakra (5th) (middle of throat)	The area of self-expression and communication; blockages manifest themselves as controlling or overpowering behavior	Turquoise blue	Thyroid and parathyroids/ upper lungs and throat
Third-eye chakra (6th) (middle of forehead)	Inner vision, self-respect, and insight, linked to the right brain; blockages can bring aimlessness and fears, and can inhibit your ability to take command of life	Indigo	Pituitary and pineal/brainstem (medulla oblongata)
Crown chakra (7th) (top of the head)	The spiritual center that helps to develop our artistic side and love of life; it can help us show kindness and compassion to others; blockages can bring isolation and even despair	Violet	Pineal/brain (cerebral cortex)

(Note: the eighth color of the spectrum, magenta, is believed to link to the aura/spirit, and not to a chakra. It is thought to affect acupuncture points, foot reflexes, and the small glands on the meridian lines.)

The chakras are positioned in the aura surrounding the physical body, along a line that corresponds to the spine.

When a chakra is adversely affected, its spinning either slows down so that it gets smaller, or speeds up so that it gets bigger. It will also do this is if a related endocrine gland or body organ is malfunctioning. People who regularly do healing treatments learn to sense through their hands whether a chakra is working at full strength or its activity is not harmonious and to treat it accordingly. You can learn to do this yourself to a certain extent, because, although the chakras are not visible to most people, if you regularly tune into or focus on the different areas where they are located, you will start to feel how well they are working. But they form a complex system, so don't worry if it takes you a while to understand their energies.

Energizing the chakras with color

A simple way to boost or rebalance the energy in a chakra that is malfunctioning is to wear some clothes of the relevant color. For example, if you are emotionally upset after a broken love affair, wearing green (the color of the heart chakra) can help to ease the pain. If you are having a problem communicating your feelings to someone, then wearing turquoise blue (the color of the throat chakra) as a scarf around your neck or even as a piece of jewelry can help to encourage freedom of self-expression.

There are several different methods described in this book – such as breathing in color (see pages 54–55), color therapy (see pages 58–61), crystal healing (see pages 66–69), and meditating with color (see pages 70–73) – whereby the colors of the chakras can be used to promote healing and balance, both emotionally and physically.

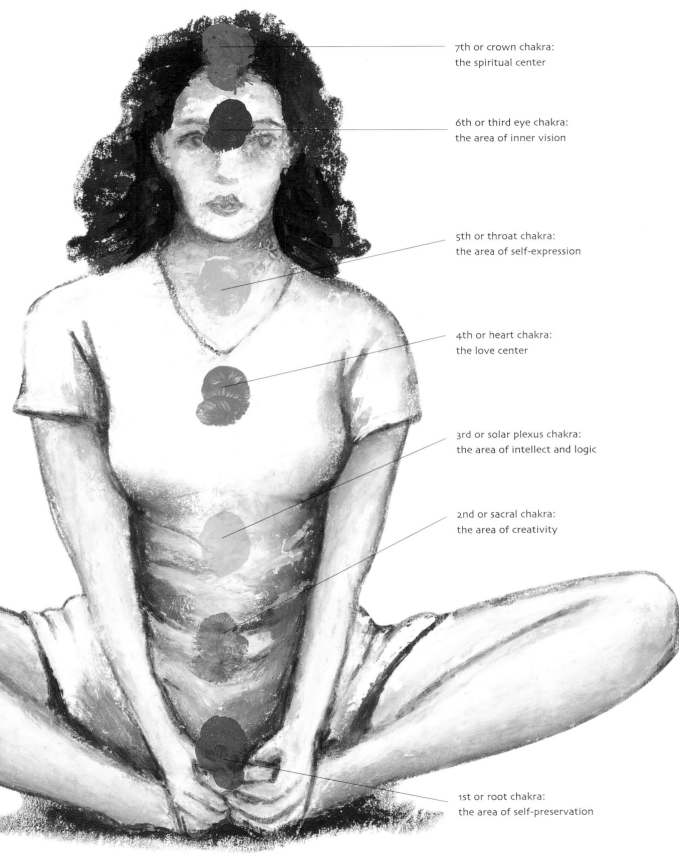

7th or crown chakra:
the spiritual center

6th or third eye chakra:
the area of inner vision

5th or throat chakra:
the area of self-expression

4th or heart chakra:
the love center

3rd or solar plexus chakra:
the area of intellect and logic

2nd or sacral chakra:
the area of creativity

1st or root chakra:
the area of self-preservation

Breathing in color

Anyone who has practiced yoga or other spiritual healing techniques will know about the benefits of deep breathing. When babies are first born, they breathe correctly from the abdomen, but as we become adults and often find ourselves under stress, we start to breathe more shallowly from the chest, using only a small percentage of our lungs' capacity. By retraining ourselves to breathe more deeply, using our diaphragm properly, we can increase the flow of energy (or *prana*, as it is known in yoga) in the body, thus improving our circulation, helping the organs to work more efficiently, and promoting a more positive mental attitude.

Once you have mastered the simple deep-breathing technique outlined below, you can then bring color into your breathing exercises. As we have seen, the chakras (the body's spiritual energy centers) and also the body's glands and organs, are influenced by different color vibrations. All light energy that is inhaled contains the seven chakra colors, so, just by breathing properly, you can take in these colors and replenish any areas in your aura that are energy-deficient, thus creating wellbeing in your physical body.

Simple deep-breathing exercise

Ideally, practice this exercise in the morning, as it may be too energizing in the evening.

Sit cross-legged on a mat on the floor or in a high-backed dining chair, with your feet firmly on the ground. Keep your spine straight, your shoulders down, and your chest open to allow for expansion of the lungs and diaphragm. Slowly inhale through your nose, breathing deeply and evenly from your abdomen for five seconds. Hold for a couple of seconds, then exhale slowly for five seconds.

Repeat the exercise for five to ten minutes, keeping your breathing balanced and even. When you have finished, you should feel quite

calm and relaxed. Practice regularly to gain the most benefit from this exercise.

Breathing-in-color exercise

Again, you should practice this exercise in the morning or early evening, so that you are not overstimulated for sleep.

Sit in the same position as for the previous exercise. You can either work intuitively, focusing on each of the chakra colors until you sense the one that your body needs, or you can make up some cards (using pens or paints of the different chakra colors) and study them closely to find the color you are lacking.

Breathe in and out deeply, as described opposite, and at the same time concentrate on your chosen color. Then, on your next breath, visualize inhaling this color; as you breathe out, feel it moving through the chakra in question, energizing this area. For instance, if your chosen color is green, see it moving through your heart chakra, removing any blockages and creating balance and harmony in this area. Repeat the procedure for five to ten minutes. Do this exercise regularly to balance the energy in your chakras.

If you are mentally upset and feel there is a disturbance in your solar plexus chakra, spend about ten minutes breathing in the color yellow to balance the energies that exist there.

Healing using the aura

Every human being is made up of a mind, body, and spirit, which need to be in balance for optimum health and harmony. To understand how therapies like color therapy (see pages 58–61) work on these levels, we need to look at the aura: the subtle energy or electro-magnetic field that surrounds the physical body. The aura is an oval shape, but its size varies, depend-ing on how spiritually aware we are. It consists of many beautiful colored layers that vibrate around our physical body. The colors that it projects reflect the state of our body, emotions, spirit, and mental health. A perfect rainbow of colors shows someone in good health.

Everyone has an invisible energy field or aura that is made of differ-ent-colored layers. The colors that we project daily show how healthy we are mentally, spiritually, and emotionally.

Auric layers

THE ETHERIC BODY

This is the layer nearest to the physical body and is closely integrated with it, but vibrates at a higher level, so it is not visible. It projects out from the body just a little, and appears rather misty. Every physical cell has an etheric double, which is why, when people have a leg amputated, they may still feel it, as its etheric form is still present. The etheric body helps to transfer life-force energy (*prana*) from the universe to the physical body.

THE ASTRAL/ EMOTIONAL BODY

As its name suggests, this second, wider layer is greatly affected by people's emotions, so it is often unbalanced. This is because one day we may feel optimistic and joyful, while the next we are depressed and anxious, and every emotion has a different energy level. These mixed emotions affect the aura's colors, so if you are emitting feelings of love, its color will be different from when you are projecting anger.

THE MENTAL BODY

This third layer is full of energy from our thoughts, and is where they become actions. Thoughts may come in dreams, from meditating, or as conscious ideas. When we think unkind thoughts about someone, these are projected as thought patterns to that person. The etheric and astral layers are also affected and filled with negativity. You will then attract back negative thought forms; conversely, if you think positively, you will attract positive thought forms.

If a picture is taken by means of aura imaging (a process that can record the energy field on film), then the person interpreting it will be able to talk to you about your present mood and aspirations. The energy that is absorbed from light rays or sunlight keeps us healthy, but if it becomes blocked, then imbalances occur in the chakras and can cause health problems.

The aura consists of several layers, but the three main ones are the etheric body, the astral/emotional body, and the mental body.

Color therapy

When color is used in healing treatments, all the colors of the spectrum are utilized: red, orange, yellow, green, turquoise, indigo, violet, and magenta. Color comes from daylight and is a form of radiation. When it is absorbed through the eyes and the skin, it has the power to heal imbalances in the body – physically, mentally, and emotionally.

As we have seen, each color has a different vibrational frequency. All the cells in the body also have a frequency that resonates strongly and positively when we are healthy; when we suffer ill health or imbalance, this frequency becomes distorted. A color therapist will choose a color that vibrates at a frequency that will bring about healing and restore your diseased cells to balance. The therapist's skill is needed to administer the correct color and quantities, as each color has both positive and negative attributes. Some therapists use both the chosen color and its complementary color on the color wheel (see right), as they feel that, in this way, they can treat the affected area more effectively.

Clinical research into color therapy has shown that it can help treat disease. For example, it has been proven that red will raise blood pressure, while blue will lower it.

Many color therapists also work with the aura (see pages 56–57) and its seven main energy centers, the chakras. If they have psychic abilities, they are often able to see deficiencies in the aura's colors. Since the chakras are all linked to a specific color (see page 51), when someone is unwell – either emotionally or physically – this will show in the color of the affected chakra.

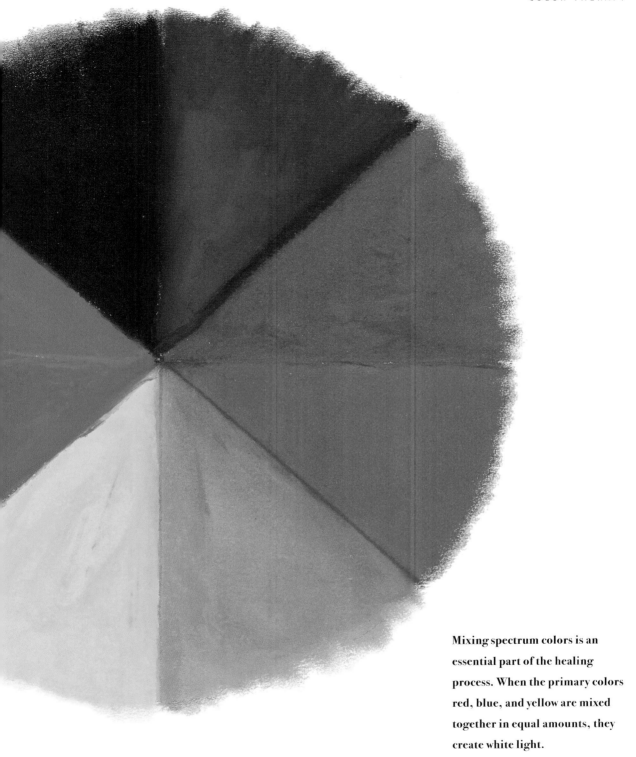

Mixing spectrum colors is an essential part of the healing process. When the primary colors red, blue, and yellow are mixed together in equal amounts, they create white light.

What happens during a treatment

When you first visit a color therapist, he or she will take details of your medical history and any current health problems. For diagnosis, therapists may use several different methods (see overleaf).

LÜSCHER TEST

This entails being shown eight colored cards; you are then asked to choose three that appeal to you. These colors relate to your emotional, mental, and physical health and may reveal imbalances that need to be corrected.

KINESIOLOGY

This involves muscle-testing techniques to identify any bodily weakness. To find out which color is needed, a therapist will normally ask you to hold up each color with your left hand, while holding your right arm horizontally across your body. As you look at each color, the therapist will gently push your right arm. When no resistance is felt in the arm, it means that you need the color you are holding.

DOWSING (see also pages 24–25)

This technique can help diagnose any colors that you are lacking. A pendulum hanging from either a cord or a chain is used and normally swings clockwise or counterclockwise in response to each question you answer with a "yes" or "no" response. The therapist works through the eight spectrum colors searching for a "yes" response to show the color you require.

COLOR DIAGNOSTIC CHART

Some therapists use this more complex method, which is based on the 32 vertebrae of the spine (see opposite). The spine is divided into four sections, each containing eight vertebrae, relating to one of the colors of the spectrum. From the top of the spine downward, the first eight vertebrae make up mental health, the second eight emotional wellbeing, the third eight metabolism, and the last eight to physical health. When therapists use this system, they ask you to sign the back of the chart along the spine. Your signature

In color diagnosis, each spinal vertebra represents both an area of health and a color that can be used to heal it.

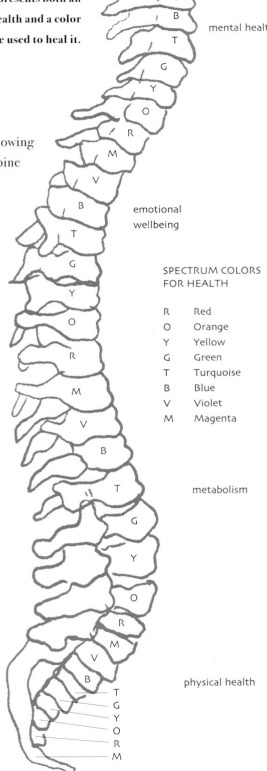

mental health

emotional wellbeing

SPECTRUM COLORS
FOR HEALTH

R	Red
O	Orange
Y	Yellow
G	Green
T	Turquoise
B	Blue
V	Violet
M	Magenta

metabolism

physical health

contains your vibration and acts as a "witness" (showing your energy). The therapist then dowses down the spine to see which vertebrae need attention.

The different treatments

Colored light is a popular method of treatment. Light is shone from a machine through stained-glass filters onto the affected part of your body. You wear a white robe throughout the session, and the therapist first carefully sets the machine so that it emits the color – and its complementary color – in the correct amounts.

Another treatment involves the therapist initially scanning your body and sensing the condition of your aura (see pages 56–57) by moving his hands up and down you. Energy blocks in the chakras (see pages 50–53) are often felt as a cold draft. You are then treated by being draped in a silk of the appropriate color and left in a bright room to absorb the maximum light. After treatment, you are covered in a silk of the complementary color to rest for 10–15 minutes. Alternatively, a lamp can be used to illuminate the treatment room with the right color. After treatment, you are bathed for a short time in light of the complementary color.

Improvement in many conditions often shows after three color treatments. Between sessions, to treat your ailment, you may be advised to wear certain colors, eat foods of these colors, or visualize them several times daily.

Aura soma therapy

As part of an aura soma treatment, you will be asked to choose colors, or color combinations, that appeal to you. This shows the therapist your inner self and how well you are functioning.

Color therapy, in the form of colored oils and herbs, is not a new technique, but can be traced back to ancient times when it was used by the Chinese, Egyptians, and Greeks to heal sickness. Aura soma is a form of color therapy invented by the late Vicky Wall, a pharmacist and chiropodist, in 1983. She had a stroke in her sixties and went blind, but, as though to compensate for her lack of sight, her inner vision developed and she became able to "see" people's auras. She also regularly had nightly visions of wonderful colors, which inspired her to create the dual-color balance bottles that are the basis of aura soma therapy. The term comes from *aura*, meaning the body's energy field, and *soma*, meaning the being within.

The colored bottles

More than 100 jewel-like bottles have now been created, each of which contains different healing properties. Unfortunately, Vicky Wall died before she could fully develop the potential of her colored oils, but her work has been carried on by the Aura Soma

Organization, which trains new therapists and regularly gives treatments to clients. The colored bottles contain a mixture of essential oils, herbs and spices, water, vegetable or herbal colorings, and crystal energies. The oils form a dual combination of non-mixing colors, with one color being present in the upper layer, while the second is contained in the lower layer of the bottle.

A gentle therapy

Aura soma is a very safe, non-intrusive therapy because it requires individuals to choose the colors that they instinctively need to bring them back into balance spiritually, mentally, emotionally, and physically. This choice determines what is explored during their consultations with the therapist. Choosing colors is highly personal – your favorite color, appealing color combinations, or colors that you currently like are all an expression of your inner self and how well it is functioning. By making your selection, you open up a medium for your soul to communicate its feelings and highlight your underlying motivations. The therapist's role is to be a helpful guide and to interpret your choices.

While aura soma therapy often heals physical disease as well, its main purpose is to address any underlying energy blockages or disturbances that are present in the aura or chakras and that can bring about illness. It is especially effective for people who are trying to bring a new focus into their life or want to develop themselves further.

Some color therapists work with the chakras and will use turquoise to balance communication or problems in the throat chakra.

What happens during treatment

The dual-colored balance bottles that you select (in what is known as a "color reading") form the key to this technique. They will help you, in your hour-long consultation, to look clearly at your current problems and what you are trying to achieve in life.

You will be asked to choose a minimum of four colored bottles from more than 100 that are currently available:

• The first bottle that you choose represents the health of your aura and the development of your spirit.

• The second bottle is connected to your past, your childhood, and any difficulties that you experienced.

• The third bottle indicates your present circumstances and your development.

• The fourth bottle shows the factors and energies that will affect your life in the near future.

After you have made your choices, the therapist will study the colored bottles to gain more information about your health and wellbeing. He or she often deduces as much from the bottles that have not been chosen as from those that have. The colored bottles, which are believed to contain an energetic healing vibration, are then used either singly or in combination for treatment. Sometimes, bottles are specially made up to match the colors of your chosen bottles. For healing, the oils in the bottles can be applied directly to the skin, or the bottles themselves may be studied visually to gain the benefits of their colors. They can also be left in different places around the home to help increase your connection with color and to help develop your intuitive instincts about their different uses. The bottles can also be incorporated into meditation practices, if you prefer.

The benefits of aura soma

Using the colored balance bottles seems to energize and create harmony in the aura by supplying the colors that are lacking or weak in it and the chakras (see pages 50–53). This therapy can relieve different types of ailments, as it is believed that we instinctively know which areas of our spirits need healing and will seek out the color or colors with the right healing vibration for the areas needing treatment. So the essences are believed to heal on all levels: repairing a damaged psyche, helping to cure physical ailments, strengthening the aura, and boosting or balancing a malfunctioning chakra. The success of treatment, however, also depends on the experience of the therapist and the accuracy and skill of his or her diagnostic abilities.

Green is a color that can balance the body; it also relates to the heart chakra and can treat diseases of the heart or love problems.

Crystal

healing

Crystal tips

Cleanse new crystals under running water for five minutes (or soak for 24 hours, if they are used for self-healing). Energize turquoise in sunlight, as water is damaging to it.

For thousands of years, crystals have been revered for their magical and healing powers, and, in today's world, the versatility of crystals in healing is becoming widely recognized. This healing power relates to the vibrational qualities emanating from the color of the crystal. When stones are placed on your body, their strong electromagnetic energies can be directed to heal blockages in chakras (see pages 50–53) or the aura (see pages 56–57) and prevent the onset of illness. By simply wearing a healing stone, such as a rose quartz crystal, you can reduce your emotional pain; or if you place one beside your bed, it can help prevent insomnia.

The essence of crystal healing

Crystals are thought to emit different healing vibrations that harmonize our internal energies, renew our body cells, and balance our auras. Clear quartz is one of the best stones known for healing, as it transmits energy known as piezoelectricity, which can accelerate the healing process. Rose quartz is good for emotional healing, while a moonstone helps to adjust the hormones.

Crystal healing is particularly successful for emotional problems, stress-related ailments, back pain, and arthritis.

What happens during a consultation

As with other therapies, the healer will ask about your health problems and will note down any drugs that you are taking. You will be asked to lie on a couch; some healers may have asked you in advance to wear white, as this color does not affect the vibrations of the crystals. The healer may well dowse your body (see pages 24–25)

The healing properties of crystals

Every crystal is believed to have its own colored energy – an electromagnetic force that can influence the chakras and affect our moods and physical wellbeing. One stone can often be substituted for another that resonates with the same color frequency, but some stones do have particular effects.

CHAKRA	COLOR	EMOTIONAL PROBLEM	CRYSTALS	BENEFITS
Root (1st)	Red	Lack of energy, no vitality for life	Bloodstone, tiger's eye, ruby	BLOODSTONE *Emotional:* improves optimism, helps decision-making *Physical:* detoxifies blood TIGER'S EYE *Emotional:* increases inner strength *Physical:* alleviates skin diseases RUBY *Emotional:* reduces mental turmoil *Physical:* treats anemia and circulatory problems

BLOODSTONE   TIGER'S EYE   RUBY

CHAKRA	COLOR	EMOTIONAL PROBLEM	CRYSTALS	BENEFITS
Sacral (2nd)	Orange	Insecurity, lack of self-worth	Amber, moonstone, carnelian	AMBER *Emotional:* promotes joy, removes negativity *Physical:* helps intestinal ailments, relieves asthma MOONSTONE *Emotional:* balances oversensitive feelings *Physical:* regulates hormones during the menstrual cycle CARNELIAN *Emotional:* gets rid of apathy, increases personal power *Physical:* improves blood disorders

AMBER   MOONSTONE   CARNELIAN

CHAKRA	COLOR	EMOTIONAL PROBLEM	CRYSTALS	BENEFITS
Solar plexus (3rd)	Yellow	Fear, stress, loss of power	Citrine, golden topaz	CITRINE *Emotional*: removes fear and promotes mental clarity *Physical*: gives a boost to the nervous system GOLDEN TOPAZ *Emotional*: relieves nervous trauma *Physical*: alleviates insomnia, protects against minor infections

CITRINE

GOLDEN TOPAZ

CHAKRA	COLOR	EMOTIONAL PROBLEM	CRYSTALS	BENEFITS
Heart (4th)	Green (rose)	Jealousy, possessive-ness, lack of tenderness	Emerald, rose quartz, aventurine	EMERALD *Emotional*: harmonizes internal feelings *Physical*: aids heart ailments, hyperten-sion, and digestion ROSE QUARTZ *Emotional*: promotes unconditional love for others *Physical*: helps to release impurities from the body AVENTURINE *Emotional*: encourages emotional wellbeing *Physical*: aids physical healing

EMERALD

ROSE QUARTZ

AVENTURINE

CHAKRA	COLOR	EMOTIONAL PROBLEM	CRYSTALS	BENEFITS
Throat (5th)	Turquoise blue	Poor commu-nication, inability to express deep feelings	Aquamarine, lapis lazuli, turquoise	AQUAMARINE *Emotional*: gives mental clarity, balances the emotions *Physical*: helps to reduce stress, protects against pollutants LAPIS LAZULI *Emotional*: encourages self-expression, helps prevent depression *Physical*: stimulates the immune system TURQUOISE *Emotional*: encourages good communication *Physical*: regulates the nervous system

AQUAMARINE

LAPIS LAZULI

TURQUOISE

CHAKRA	COLOR	EMOTIONAL PROBLEM	CRYSTALS	BENEFITS
Third eye (6th)	Indigo	Indecisiveness, poor intuition, lack of imagination	Amethyst, fluorite, sodalite	AMETHYST *Emotional*: deepens spiritual awareness, can be transformational *Physical*: can relieve headaches, helps with insomnia FLUORITE *Emotional*: releases emotional blockages *Physical*: clears headaches, can give body cells a boost SODALITE *Emotional*: can encourage you to find new objectives *Physical*: helps reduce deep-rooted pain

AMETHYST   FLUORITE   SODALITE

CHAKRA	COLOR	EMOTIONAL PROBLEM	CRYSTALS	BENEFITS
Crown (7th)	Violet, white, and gold	Lack of spiritual awareness, fear of being unprotected, searching for more wisdom	Celestite, clear quartz, milky quartz	CELESTITE *Emotional*: awakens spirituality, increases vitality *Physical*: relieves headaches CLEAR QUARTZ *Emotional*: a powerful crystal that encourages purity, aids meditation *Physical*: good for pain relief MILKY QUARTZ *Emotional*: takes away resentment, produces creativity *Physical*: encourages body cleansing

CELESTITE   CLEAR QUARTZ   MILKY QUARTZ

with a quartz pendulum to find blockages in your chakras. Some healers may ask it if there is a blockage and obtain a "yes" or "no" response, while others will simply let the pendulum swing clockwise or counterclockwise, as is normal for the chakra (this varies for men and women). Wide swings indicate that the chakra is open; irregular swings show a blockage.

The healer may then treat with the relevant stone (see chart) specific areas where there is pain or a chakra blockage. He or she may also place single crystals on each chakra in order to conduct a full treatment, or crystals may be placed on the meridians (the inner channels of energy). Some patients fall asleep during the session, as it is very relaxing. You may end up taking crystals home with you so that you can treat yourself. Some improvement in your condition should be felt after about three treatments.

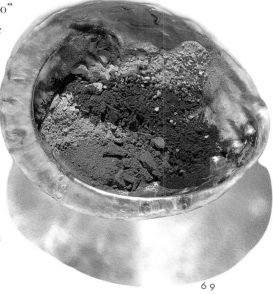

Meditating with color

When you are meditating to rebalance the chakras, sit comfortably in a high-backed chair to support your spine and focus initially on the color red seeping into your root chakra.

Meditation is a process that can help relax the mind and bring about a calm and peaceful mental state. It can heal on all levels, opening up the mind to different types of consciousness. The discipline has been in practice for more than 4,000 years and is strongly associated with the Buddhist and Hindu religions, and with yoga. Meditation can help us manage our busy thought processes, leave behind our worries and fears, slow down our bodily functions, and let us be taken away from our egos so that we can commune with our subconscious and the spiritual world that is deep within us. Here we can feel joy, bliss, and be at one with ourselves.

Types of meditation

There are different forms of meditation:
• Transcendental meditation, which involves mentally repeating a specific word or mantra (sacred word)
• Meditation with spiritual forms, such as a mandala (a circular design symbolizing the universe)
• Meditation while focusing on an object such as a candle
• Meditation and deep breathing (*pranayama*)
• Meditation with visualization – when you focus on visualizing the chakra colors, this form of meditation can be extremely powerful, influencing you emotionally, spiritually, and physically.

Meditation can alleviate various conditions, but especially stress and stress-related illnesses, such as asthma or high blood pressure.

Practicing meditation

When you want to meditate, find somewhere that is quiet and away from traffic noise and other distractions. Try to use the same place time after time, so that you build up good energy vibrations there,

which will make it easier for you to meditate there. To create the right atmosphere, surround yourself with energizing crystals, incense, icons and images of spiritual teachers, and perhaps some fresh flowers.

When you first start meditating, do it for ten minutes daily (ideally in the morning) and gradually build up to 20 minutes. Try to keep to a regular time in order to discipline yourself. Don't become distressed if you find it hard to concentrate and keep getting distracted, as meditation requires regular practice. When you have finished meditating, it is a good idea to close down your chakras (see pages 50–53), as they will have opened fully during the process. Imagine each one as an open flower that is closing its petals. Start at the top with the crown chakra, working down through the third eye, throat, heart, solar plexus, and sacral chakra, until you reach the root chakra.

When you visualize the different colors of the chakras during meditation, you can clear blockages and create harmony in your body.

Simple energizing meditation

This brief visualization meditation can lift your energy or help you solve a problem.

Either sit cross-legged on the floor on a mat, with your spine straight, or on a high-backed dining chair with both feet firmly on the ground. Close your eyes and relax by breathing in and out deeply and evenly. As you exhale, breathe out any existing tension. Then imagine yourself surrounded by sunlight that radiates from within you. Relish this light; feel its warmth and strength. Let the image grow stronger for a few minutes, then slowly come to and open your eyes. Practice this regularly for a week and notice the changes in you.

Using the chakra colors

The more practiced you become at meditation, the more you can use it to balance your physical and spiritual energies. By bringing color into your meditation, you can treat any minor physical problems that you are experiencing. For instance, backache can be relieved by visualizing orange or red in the lower back area; if the pain is all over your back, visualize all the chakra colors moving up and down your spine. Visualizing the complementary color (see page 58) can balance the energy you are receiving.

Meditation to protect your aura

For this meditation, you need to do the simple energizing meditation (see page 71) first, then choose either the color white or gold (colors of the crown chakra) as your focus. Or try the meditation first with the color white, and then with gold, and see which one makes you feel safest. Practice for about ten minutes just before you get up or go to sleep in order to protect your aura and repel any negativity.

If you are suffering from stomach ache, visualize the warmth of the color of the solar plexus chakra filling the area between your abdomen and breastbone and easing the pain.

Sit as for the Simple Energizing Meditation and take two or three deep breaths, slowly and evenly. Then concentrate on relaxing all of your muscles, starting at your feet, working up through your knees and thighs, and breathing steadily as you release any pent-up tension. Now concentrate on your stomach, chest, shoulders, spine, and neck, noticing how different your muscles feel as they relax. Next work on your arms, and then slowly move up to your face, letting go of any stiffness in your jaw. Now visualize a bright light above your head and feel it surrounding your body, entering every cell and giving it nourishment. Let your body be overwhelmed with love and contentment.

Stay with the feeling for a few moments, then close your eyes and imagine the light of your chosen color extending all around your body. Expand or contract its shape until you feel happy with its size. Feel protected by it. To finish, close down your chakras, then open your eyes.

Rebalancing the chakras

You can use part of this meditation to focus on just one chakra (see pages 50–53), by visualizing its color. Or do the whole meditation, working through all the chakras to create a feeling of harmony. Take about ten minutes to do the meditation.

Sit as described for the Simple Energizing Meditation. Close your eyes and breathe deeply. Relax all your muscles. Focus your attention on your lower spine and pelvic area, the root chakra. Visualize the color red seeping into these areas, then experience its warmth as it goes down your legs to your feet and connects you to the earth. Sense the release of insecure feelings, welcoming stability into your life.

Now concentrate on your sacral chakra, in your abdomen just below your navel. Visualize the color orange moving through this area, nourishing your stomach, kidneys, and bladder, and your reproductive organs. This is the area of sexual pleasure, so release any stress that may be restricting your sensual feelings or general wellbeing.

Moving on to your solar-plexus chakra, situated between your abdomen and breastbone, visualize a strong yellow color filling this area, boosting your self-confidence. See it soothing any tension in your stomach and helping to release toxins from your liver.

Now center your attention on your heart chakra, in the upper chest. Visualize the color green flowing through this area and traveling down your arms and hands. Take a few minutes to feel the warmth of this energy as it slows your breathing, calms your heart, and fills you with sensations of love and peace.

Next move to your throat chakra, situated over the middle of your throat. Visualize a turquoise blue flooding your jawbone, throat, and neck, easing any tension there. Don't worry if you cough a little; you are shifting blockages.

For the third-eye chakra in the center of your forehead, visualize a deep indigo color moving into your eyes, ears, mouth, and brain, relaxing the activity of your mind. Listen to any intuitive thoughts as the energy comes into this area.

Finally, move on to the crown chakra on top of your head, and visualize the color violet permeating your body. Feel how it calms you and gives you serenity as you connect to your spiritual self. Shut down the chakras and slowly open your eyes.

One of the best positions for meditating is sitting cross-legged in the lotus position. Keep your spine straight, close your eyes, and relax.

73

Dreaming
in color

For years, people have been fascinated by the symbolism of dreams and their interpretation. Our ancestors believed that dreams contained messages that could solve problems. We tend to dream most nights, but generally we do not realize the importance of these regular night-time experiences. In our dreams, we can eavesdrop on discussions between our conscious and subconscious mind, which will help us to find out more about ourselves and achieve inner harmony and balance.

However, scientific analysis of dreams is barely 50 years old. William Dement, a psychologist working at the University of Chicago, found, during his research, a connection between a dream's contents and the psychological state of the dreamer. He established that most people recall only about 80 percent of their dreams, if they wake immediately afterward. This recall rapidly deteriorates, falling to about 30 percent in the next ten minutes or so of being awake. Current research is trying to understand the content of dreams, looking at their creative input, and how they are influenced by experiences before sleep.

A time to dream

Most of the dreams that we remember happen during what is known as Rapid Eye Movement (REM) sleep, when activity behind the closed eyes can be detected and there are noticeable changes in the brain's electrical rhythms. REM sleep first occurs (for a period of about five minutes) about an hour or so after falling asleep. Three or even four further periods of REM sleep usually occur during a normal night's sleep (generally about ten minutes apart), with each period lasting longer than the previous one. The final dreaming session can last for as long as 30–35 minutes. Total REM dreaming lasts for about 80 minutes.

Many of our dreams contain color to give us some guidance in our lives. Orange can represent ambition, pink a need for love, yellow a rational approach, green the need for healing, while blue shows hope for the future.

We need REM sleep to keep psychologically healthy. If deprived of sleep, we suffer from memory loss, fatigue, lack of concentration, and general irritability. Many scientists agree that dreaming is valuable, but often dismiss its jumbled content as meaningless. Other researchers disagree, observing that through recurring dreams, the surfacing of old memories, and the interpretation of dreams, we may gain therapeutic benefits and useful guidance.

Symbols in dreams

The majority of messages that we receive in dreams seem to come as symbols, representing an idea or emotion that we are trying to express. Once we understand these symbols, we can begin to see how meaningful our dreams are. The reason why symbols are so

apparent in dreams is that the dream state is connected with the subconscious mind, and that is how it communicates. Many symbols are personal to each dreamer, but others have universal messages:

• A bird represents freedom
• A dog indicates loyalty and faithfulness
• Fire represents destruction
• A funeral denotes the ending of a phase.

Dream colors and positions

Colors appear in your dreams to bring healing or guidance to your life. When more passive shades (such as black, gray, or brown) are seen, these reflect your fears about following any advice you have been given. If you see pink (perhaps in a room setting) and a very green garden, then the dream is trying to bring more love and harmony into your life.

When negative shades of color are worn by an unpleasant male character, this can indicate bad attributes that you have copied from your father. For example, if someone wears a black coat, it can mean that you have adopted his fear of the world. When negative shades are worn by an unpleasant female character, it shows the detrimental effect that your mother had upon you.

The position of colors in a dream is also important. When they appear on the floor, they are representing emotions within yourself that you need to overcome. Colors that appear high up on a wall or in the sky relate to ideals for which you need to aim. The colors will generally relate to the chakras (see pages 50–53) and their current energy, but other colors may also appear (including cream, brown, and black) and these are interpreted differently. The chart opposite summarizes the basic meanings and interpretations of colors in dreams.

The color in your dreams

COLOR	CHAKRA	BASIC MEANING	INTERPRETATION
White	Crown	Purity, perfection, hope	Indicates a rigid and judgmental attitude
Black	–	Fear, anxiety, guilt, resentment	Holding on to fear, lack of faith in the future
Red	Root	Joy, sexuality, passion, fun	Lack of fun in life; combined with black, red indicates anger; with white, it shows a need for hope for the future
Orange	Sacral	Drive, ambition	A move forward in career dreams
Yellow	Solar plexus	Intellect, rationality	Can represent the dreamer's visual reaction to what she is seeing; if yellow is represented on an unhelpful character, it can mean difficulty in solving a problem
Green	Heart	Healing, harmony, balance	Dark green can show difficulties in sharing; otherwise it indicates the heart becoming more open emotionally
Pink	Heart	Love, need for unconditional love	Can mean the dreamer did not bond with his or her mother, or lacked love as a baby
Blue	Throat	Philosophy, spirituality, cultural aspirations	Dark blue can represent a negative view of life; light blue or turquoise shows hope and faith in the future
Purple (violet/indigo/lilac)	Crown, third eye	Spiritual teaching or leadership	Violet can show endurance in all things; lilac means taking responsibility for your life; indigo represents clairvoyance
Cream	–	Acceptance	Represents a growing maturity, a new tolerance
Gray	–	No commitment	Can represent denial of emotion, depression
Brown	–	Practical attitude	An unenlightened attitude to life, denial of the spiritual side

Reiki healing with color

The word reiki can be broken down into two parts: "*rei*", meaning the universal side of energy, and "*ki*", meaning the life-force energy that exists in every living thing. Reiki is an ancient, hands-on healing technique that was revived in the mid-nineteenth century by Dr Mikao Usui in Japan. In reiki, the healer channels the life-force energy, which goes where it is needed in the body and stimulates the body's natural healing ability to remove any blockages that have been causing illness or discomfort. During treatment, the body is cleansed of toxins, and balance is brought to the chakras (see pages 50–53), creating overall harmony.

Stress-related illness, backache, migraine, and chronic conditions such as asthma or eczema all respond well to reiki.

The attunements

To practice reiki, a healer needs to be attuned with a reiki master to receive the universal life-force energy. In first-degree reiki (which is for people who want to treat themselves and their friends) in the Usui system, initiation – which often takes place over a weekend – consists of four attunements to open the heart, hand (not part of the major chakra system), and crown chakras.

Second-degree reiki initiation, again taking place over a weekend, is for people who want to practice reiki. A further attunement is received in order to strengthen energy flow, together with the reiki symbols, which can be used for mental and emotional healing, as well as absent healing.

With third-degree reiki, you become a master and can then attune other people. A further symbol and mantra are given, and another attunement increases the energy you have. This can be a year-long apprenticeship, or it can be done in two parts.

What happens during treatment

On a first visit, a reiki healer will ascertain what problems you are trying to improve and note any medication that you are receiving.

You will be asked to lie fully clothed on a couch for the hour-long healing session. The healer will scan your body for imbalances, which may be felt as a cold draft. He or she will then work on four head positions while sitting behind you. For the next four body positions on your chest and lower body, the healer will stand. The healing energy is often felt as heat or a tingling sensation. You will then be asked to turn over for the last four positions on your shoulders and back, by which time you will feel very relaxed. To finish the treatment, the healer will "ground" you, moving the energy back up your body.

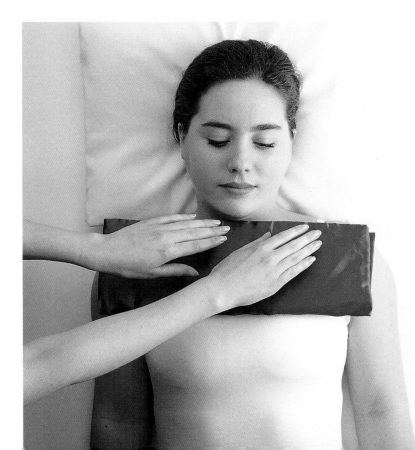

To treat a chakra, the healer places a piece of colored silk over the relevant area so that the color vibrations intensify the effects of the reiki healing. Here, the throat chakra is being treated with turquoise.

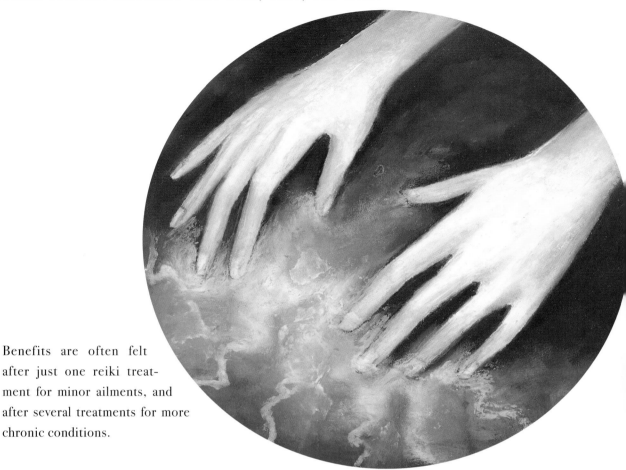

Benefits are often felt
after just one reiki treatment for minor ailments, and
after several treatments for more
chronic conditions.

Combining color with reiki

To intensify the effects of reiki treatment, it can be combined with
color therapy to cure a disturbance in a specific chakra and in turn
heal any physical problems that exist, or balance the whole energy
system. The vibrating frequencies that come from the spectrum
of colors linked to the chakras (see pages 50–53) work with reiki
energy to produce powerful results.

The therapist will use silk squares (or something similar), which
are about 6 in. x 6 in. (15cm x 15cm) square, as these are the easiest
items to apply. If one chakra needs particular attention, then a silk
square will be placed over that area; alternatively, seven squares in all
the different chakra colors will be positioned over the chakra areas
(see chart opposite) and then the healer's hands will go on top during a full-body treatment, during which five minutes is spent in each
position. If the material moves around a lot, then the healer may
decide to treat you by holding his or her hands above your body. This
technique is just as effective, and you will still receive the color
vibrations, but it is operating in the aura (etheric body).

The therapist's hands channel life-force energy to the body, clearing blockages and stimulating its innate healing abilities.

Treating the chakras with reiki and color

A full-body reiki treatment always starts with the head, so the chakras below are listed from the top downward.

CHAKRA	POSITION	COLOR	WHAT IT CAN HELP
Crown (7th)	Top of the head HEALER'S HANDS: over the head covering the eyes REIKI POSITION: first	Violet (white or gold)	Being upset about life, a lack of spiritual connection
Third eye (6th)	Middle of forehead HEALER'S HANDS: at the side of the head REIKI POSITION: second	Indigo	Confusion, stress, irritability, headaches, insomnia
Throat (5th)	Middle of throat HEALER'S HANDS: over the jaw-bone covering the throat area. REIKI POSITION: fourth	Turquoise blue	Throat problems, tonsillitis, speaking the truth; relieves anger, hostility, and resentment
Heart (4th)	Center of the chest over the heart HEALER'S HANDS: on top of chest below neck REIKI POSITION: fifth	Green or rose	Functioning of the immune system and circulation; problems in expressing love or dealing with sensitive issues
Solar plexus (3rd)	Upper abdomen HEALER'S HANDS: on abdomen, below the chest REIKI POSITION: sixth and seventh	Yellow	Stomach problems and digestion; depression, fears, and nervous-system upsets
Sacral (2nd)	Pelvic area HEALER'S HANDS: over the lower abdomen REIKI POSITION: seventh and eighth	Orange	Kidney and bladder ailments; sexual dysfunction; bitter or negative feelings
Root (1st)	Base of spine HEALER'S HANDS: either side of the groin REIKI POSITION: eighth	Red (use a soft red, as bright red is too energizing)	Constipation or diarrhea; lack of enthusiasm, energy, or creativity

Creating color harmony in the home

CONTENTS

Color vibrations directly affect both our emotional and physical wellbeing, and they also influence how happily we live in our homes. The color that emanates from our walls has the power to make us feel content, calm, or inspired to socialize. Conversely, unsuitable colors can make us feel unsettled, restless, and unsure about the future.

A spiritual approach to achieving color harmony uses the Five Element system – an integral part of Compass School feng shui. Each of the elements – Wood, Water, Earth, Fire, and Metal – has a special energy, and is associated with a color and one or more compass directions. In this last section, you can use this system to change the atmosphere, improve family relations, and transform your life for the better.

Using color in the home

We can walk into a room and instantly fall in love with its color or take an active dislike to it. This is because color vibrates at different frequencies and creates a reaction in all of us.

To bring about harmony and balance in each room of your home, you can choose wallpaper or paint colors for walls using the ancient principles of the Five Elements in feng shui (see pages 38–41). Each feng shui element relates to one or more compass directions, and, by linking each room to its elemental color, you can tap into the positive chi (energy) of that space to make it a more comfortable and pleasant place to live. Generally, the perception is that the darker the color, such as black or blue, then the more yin (passive) it is. The lighter

The Five Elements and their colors

Here is a reminder of the colors and directions that relate to the Five Elements:

ELEMENT	DIRECTION	COLOR
Water	North	Blue (black)
Fire	South	Red
Wood	East, southeast	Green
Metal	West, northwest	White (metal and gold)
Earth	Northeast, southwest	Yellow (beige)

Soft, draping pink curtains help to make this room a healing sanctuary.

Bedlinen in a soft lemon shade will bring some calming energy.

A pink carpet tones well, bringing in yin Fire energy.

A healing rose quartz crystal by the bed will aid sleep.

the color, such as white, the more yang (positive) it is. An exception is red, which is considered a very yang color. Darker or brighter shades of a color bring in more energy, while softer, pastel shades generate less energy. However, it is more important to find the one shade of a color that appeals most to you – your own special shade that you will always love. So look through several different color charts, and try out numerous sample paint pots, until you find your own particular shade.

Obviously, for the Five Element system to work effectively, you may need to change the color of all the rooms in your home, plus your hall, to their matching elements (ceilings can be left white because they are considered neutral). This takes time, so do pace yourself. If, for example, you know that you can't paint a room for a while, you can create some of its element's color by using furnishings and accessories of the color, so that you can still enjoy some of its beneficial energy until you redecorate.

Find the Fire color that suits you. Here, in a bedroom, the color used is violet. Try to choose natural materials for your bedroom, such as muslin, cotton, and wood for furniture, and keep the room free from electro-magnetic stress caused by digital alarm clocks, televisions, and electric blankets.

Compass readings

When you go around your home with your compass, you may find that in some doorways you are getting inconsistent readings because of concealed iron or steel beams, water or gas pipes, or electrical appliances. If this happens, walk further back into the room, still facing the direction of the energy, and try in several areas until the compass gives consistent readings.

Using the compass

When a feng shui consultant visits you, she will often use an expensive Chinese compass, or *Lo P'an*, to map out your home. However, for you to find out your rooms' directions and elements, all you need is a standard orienteering compass.

Start at the front door, standing in your hall facing the door, and adjust the compass until the pointer is on magnetic north (if north is marked red, make sure that you align the red pointer with it) checking the direction that lies ahead of you. If, for example, the red pointer is on north (to the left) and the white pointer is on south (to the right), then straight ahead is east – the direction of Wood, and the color to match the element of your hall and front door should, therefore, be green (study the box on page 84 to find which element colors are relative to the various compass directions). If you have a house with several floors, paint the stairwells and connecting hallways in the same color as the direction of the energy that comes in the front door.

Stand at the door to your room looking out to take a compass reading. This measures the direction from which chi energy is entering the room.

Mark all these directions down on a pad and then go around each room in your home, noting down the different directions and elements. Always stand in the doorway, with your back to the room, to find its direction; you want to establish the direction from which the energy is entering the room, not the direction that it faces.

Using the Pa Kua

Once your room is decorated, you may want to find your eight aspirational areas using the feng shui diagnostic tool, the Pa Kua. On some graph paper, draw a plan of your room to scale. From each corner, draw two diagonal lines that meet in the center, and place your compass here so that you can mark off the different directions, using your initial reading from the door (see page 86). Use the color compass, or photocopy the Pa Kua here to the right size and place it on the plan. Match the directions, then write in the aspirational areas. To boost these areas, you can use the following accessories:

DIRECTION/ELEMENT/ASPIRATIONS	ACCESSORIES
South, Fire, Recognition, and fame	Lights, candles
Southwest, Earth, Marriage, and relationships	Paired items: candles, hearts, ducks, and statues
West, Metal, Children	Metal statues, electrical equipment
Northwest, Metal, Mentors, and networking	Hollow metal windchimes
North, Water, Career	Aquarium or other water feature (but not in bedrooms or kitchens: use blue ornaments there)
Northeast, Earth, Education, and knowledge	Crystals: clear quartz, amethyst, rose quartz
East, Wood, Family, and health	Houseplants with rounded leaves (but not in bedrooms: use wooden items there)
Southeast, Wood, Wealth, and prosperity	Water fountains, money, jade, plants (but not in bedrooms: use wooden bowls containing coins there)

The Fire element

TRIGRAM: Li
DIRECTION: south
COLOR: red
ASPIRATION: recognition and fame
SEASON: summer

Fire has always been seen as extremely powerful — from ancient times, the sight of roaring flames filled people with awe. It has a tangible, raw energy that you can almost feel. In feng shui terms, the element of Fire is linked to the heat of summer and the color red: a passionate, vibrant, and stimulating color that is believed to bring good fortune and happiness, but a color that can also profoundly affect our moods, giving shy people more courage, but causing aggression and anger if used too strongly. Red also has the ability to affect the heart and circulatory system, and to increase blood pressure. A sensual and warm color that is full of yang (positive) stimulating energy, it can make a powerful impact on a room.

Red can light up the southern part of your home or a room in the south. It relates to your Fame sector, which is an important part of the Pa Kua; it is about your talent (often in the workplace), about recognition, and how you are viewed in the world. By enhancing the element of this area, you are harmonizing the flow of chi and encouraging public acknowledgment of the achievements of all family members.

The passion of red

Red is also about romance and sexuality, and it stimulates physical love, so shades of red can add vibrancy to your bedroom if it has a southern orientation or is in the south of your home. However, do resist using too intense a shade, or you may find that either the red is too overwhelming, or that your passion starts to wane. This color is also good for rooms in the south that lack natural light, as the red will bring warmth and movement. Rooms that usually have a lot of activity, such as hallways or playrooms, respond well to the stimulation of red —a rich red dining room looks sumptuous and inviting in the evening, encouraging long, lingering meals with convivial, lively conversation.

This mirror will reflect the food served on the table and symbolically double the size of the meal.

Candles create the right ambience for dining and add to the yang Fire energy of the dining room.

Wood flooring brings stimulating energy into this room.

A round wooden table is the most auspicious. It represents the Wood element, which feeds the room's element, Fire.

Red fabric emphasizes the Fire element, while the chairs' high backs give people support and protection when eating.

Energy vibrations

The stronger and purer the red wallpaper or paint that you use in a room, the more Fire vibrations you will bring into it. However, always choose a shade that appeals to your soul, something that enriches your being whenever you look at it. Whether you choose a bright tomato red, a brown terra-cotta, a soft pink, or a rich orange – you need to love the shade, but also be able to live with it. Reactions to colors are intensely personal, so you must use what appeals to you.

For a dining room in the south, which is linked to the Fire element, reds are perfect for creating cozy comfort, whereas the natural wood table and floor support Fire in the Five Element Cycle (see page 93).

The yin and yang of Fire

The shade of red that you choose denotes the level of Fire energy that you are bringing into your southern room or area. It also shows the strength of the energy – whether it is yang (positive) or more yin (passive). Looking at the colors shown here, the deep, bright tomato red is the strongest yang Fire color, while the soft pink shade is the most yin color. So, in a south kitchen, a bright, strong yang red will energize this vibrant, sociable room, but the weaker energies

YANG REDS

of a soft yin pink or peachy-pink shade will suit a bathroom better, where energy is weak, or a bedroom, as this is an oasis where your spirit rests. Do think carefully about very soft pink shades in other rooms located in the south, as the red vibrations are much lower because of the mix with white, the color of Metal, which clashes with Fire in the Element Cycle.

The different varieties of red

Dark, bright reds and their lighter versions send out the most positive energy into Fire rooms. However, such colors can feel too strong, and there are many other tones of red that may appeal to you more.

Tip

Painting the front door

The chi first enters through the front door—the "mouth" of your home—so it is important when using the elemental color system that this door is painted the correct color to ensure a positive flow. For a Fire entrance, bright red is the best color, or you can bring in even more energy with a deep green, as Wood produces Fire in the Element Cycle.

ORANGE

This carries the heat of red, but less intensely. It is a creative, exciting color that is uplifting in a hall or dining room. A combination of red and yellow in the element cycle, it emits calming Earth energy. Softer versions are rust, terra-cotta, peach, and apricot.

MAROON

Maroon is a deep, darker shade of red that has a cocooning warmth. It still carries a strong amount of fiery energy. Its vibrations are not

YIN REDS

quite as strong as a bright tomato red, because it contains some black, one of the Water colors, which in the element cycle destroys Fire. Its richness can suit late eating in a dining room, but may feel too heavy in a hallway.

MAUVE, PURPLE, AND VIOLET

These colors relate to Fire energy, but are a mixture of blue and red, so some of their energy is destroyed by the blue of the Water element. They are nurturing, balancing, and protective shades, but are not so stimulating as other Fire colors, so are not ideal for a Fire kitchen. They can draw out your intuitive side in a study, and be relaxing in a living room.

The shade of red you choose denotes the level of Fire energy you bring into your home. Deep reds bring in the most yang energy, while soft pinks bring in yin energy.

Colors to energize or calm Fire

If you want to do more than enhance the existing energy in your Fire room or area, you can bring in stimulating green (as Wood produces Fire in the Element Cycle). So choose the shade of green that most appeals to you (see pages 110–111).

Conversely, in other south rooms, a relaxing atmosphere may be more appropriate. For example, if you want your living room to be your sanctuary, decorate in shades of yellow or beige (see pages 120–121), as Earth calms Fire in the Element Cycle.

The different Fire colors and their actions

ROOM ELEMENT	COLOR	WHAT IT DOES
FIRE	Red	Strengthens energy
Producing (feeding) Element Wood	Green	Energizes Fire (good for rooms in which you are busy and creative)
Exhausting (calming) Element Earth	Yellow (beige)	Calms Fire energy (good for rooms in which you relax)
Destroying (controlling) Element Water	Blue (black)	Extinguishes Fire energy
Clashing Element Metal	White (metal and gold)	Takes away Fire energy

92

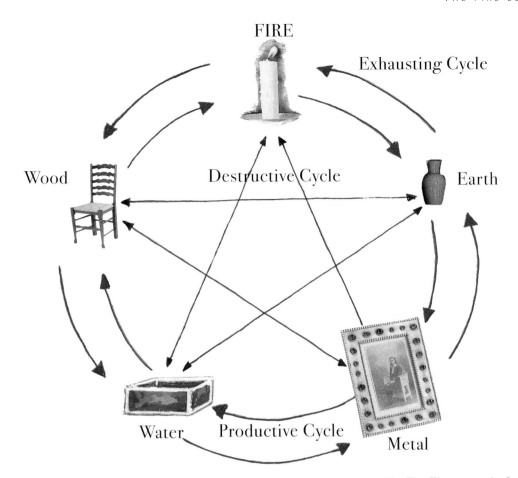

FIRE

Exhausting Cycle

Wood

Destructive Cycle

Earth

Water

Productive Cycle

Metal

Conflicting colors

When you use the Five Element system in your home, there are also colors that are best kept to a minimum in the different rooms, depending on their orientation. The element of Water destroys Fire in the Element Cycle, so the colors blue and black should, ideally, appear only in small quantities in your color scheme or furnishings, because they can disrupt a room's ambience. The Metal element, which links to white, metal, and gold, also clashes with Fire, so again keep these colors to a minimum; just incorporate them as accents.

You can occasionally use a conflicting energy to control a situation. For instance, if you have a disruptive child and nothing you do seems to stop him or her playing up, then you can try featuring the destroying element color on their bedclothes to weaken the energy in that area. So in a Fire bedroom that is painted pink, changing the quilt to a blue color could help to calm the temper tantrums. This same treatment could also work for a disagreeable or bad-tempered partner; you could even apply the destroying colors to a cat or dog's bedding, if they were being unruly or causing you other problems.

The Five Element cycle shows the interaction of the elements. For vibrancy, boost Fire energy with greens (Wood), which feed Fire in the Element Cycle, or create a serene atmosphere with Earth colors. Generally, avoid using Water (blues) and Metal colors (white, gold, and silver), which conflict with Fire.

Accessorizing a Fire room

After choosing the shade of red for your south room or area, you can plan the accessories, soft furnishings, and furniture to harmonize, calm, or boost the Fire energy. If you have used green to boost the energy, add some Wood items or include some Fire accessories. If you have calmed the energy with yellow, then display some Earth (see page 124–25) or Fire accessories.

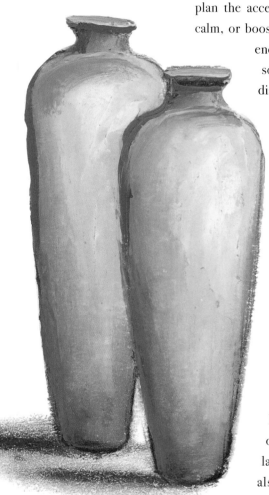

Green ceramics, such as decorative vases or lamp bases, or green, round-leaved plants, all add extra stimulus to the existing energy of a Fire room.

How to energize

To create stimulating energy in your Fire room, incorporate some wooden or green accessories. In an open-plan living room, a round or oval wooden dining table will energize the diners and make them linger for longer. Square and rectangular tables are also fine, provided no one sits at the corners. Wicker, bamboo, or rattan storage units and round side-tables also increase the energy in living and dining areas. These units stop Water energy from draining out of bathrooms, but too many of them in a Fire bedroom can disturb its peace.

Small wooden decorative items, such as candle-holders, picture frames, carved bowls, Oriental boxes, or statues, can be dotted around living areas. Green lamps, ceramic bowls, plant pots, and ornaments will also add to the boosting effect in all Fire rooms. Houseplants are also the Wood element. Round-leaved varieties, such as peperomias and goosefoot plants, are great for lifting the atmosphere and filtering pollutants, but avoid plants in bedrooms because they are too yang. In a Fire kitchen, they fuel a positive atmosphere, while in a Fire bathroom they fight the conflict there between Fire and Water.

Harmonizing your Fire room

You can also accentuate the energies in your south room by including some Fire accessories. Red or pink bowls, vases, candlesticks
and candles, ornaments, red flowers or flowering plants will all
add to the room's style. Adding touches of the
calming and stimulating energies creates yin and
yang balance.

   Each of the Five Elements is also linked to
a shape, and in the case of Fire, it is the triangular
shape. So, in order to further strengthen the room's
atmosphere, you can bring in zigzag, diamond, star, or
pyramid designs via soft furnishings, carpets, or rugs.

**Look out for unusual designs that
reflect the triangle, the shape of
the Fire element. A triangular
cushion in rich orange gives
impetus to Fire energy.**

Drapes and fabrics

When planning your drape treatments, keep the Fire symbol in
mind. If you are having a pelmet made, the design can include triangular sections, although be careful about placing seating under-
neath pelmets, because bad sha chi (negative energy) can come off
the points and negatively affect the people sitting there. Use a
blending shade of red or pink material to match the decor of the
room, and perhaps include a delicate star or zigzag pattern.

   Soft furnishings can be chosen in the same way, but you may
decide that you want the energy from the throws on your sofas, for
example, to calm you. So in a Fire living room, choose throw fabrics
in shades of yellow (because Earth calms Fire in the Element Cycle)
– with a checked or striped pattern, if you like. With the fabric on
your cushions, you may want more stimulating energy, so pick a
shade of green with a pattern of vertical stripes (because Wood produces Fire in the Element Cycle). Alternatively, have yellow blending
cushions and just incorporate an energizing green and harmonizing

**The triangle of the Fire element
can be used in subtle, modern
motifs on ceramics and borders.**

Candles have a romantic ambience of their own, and bring soft Fire energy into a room.

red in their pattern. It is best to be more subtle with the shade of red accessories in a bedroom, because they can be too energizing – soft pink or peach bedspreads and duvet sets are preferable.

Rich, red upholstery with rounded arms creates luxurious comfort and enhances the Fire energy in a south room.

The right furniture

In a living area, sumptuous deep-red sofas and chairs in tactile fabrics, such as velvets and silks, can make a room more appealing. Rounded sofa arms are more yin and relaxing, and encourage comfort. In a dining room that is regularly used for dinner parties, high-backed chairs with red or pink loose covers or upholstery will fuel the appetites of dinner guests. A home study or office needs to have a motivating atmosphere that encourages you to settle and concentrate, so a high red office chair will provide support and aid mental inspiration.

Floor treatments

The colors of your carpet can be chosen in the same way as described above, although, to maximize the room's energy, you should, ideally, choose a shade of red – a soft pink or even a pinky-beige often blends well with a stronger red on the walls.

**Zigzag patterns add to the energy
of a Fire room – look for this in
Eastern-style or ultra-modern
rugs and carpets.**

Wooden flooring brings more warmth into the room and will not
stagnate the flow of energy as a carpet does, but bear in mind
that it introduces stimulating energy, which is not ideal if
you want a really serene room.

Decorative rugs can create a good focal point in a
room, particularly when laid over neutral carpets or
plain wooden flooring. Kilims and Turkish or
Oriental-style rugs often feature triangular
and zigzag patterns in their design that will
suit a Fire room. Alternatively, a bold,
modern rug with stripes in red and yellow, or yellow and green, will
also work well. You can introduce a small amount of blue and white
in patterns, but do remember that these colors do not work so well
with the Fire element because they destroy or clash with Fire in
the Element Cycle.

Lighting

Lamps and candles are also the Fire
element, and their active, yang
energy can instill more warmth
and vibrancy in a south room.
Choose tall lamps with wooden or metal
stands to create pools of light in dull, dark corners in living areas,
while in a bedroom, small bedside lamps with pink shades give a soft
glow that will not overwhelm the sense of tranquility that is needed.
Spotlights or downlighters in a bathroom will lift the slow yin energy
that exists there. Candles are softer Fire energy – they have a special,
indefinable mystery, adding atmosphere to living areas, romance
to the bedroom or dining room, and lifting the slow, humid mood
of the bathroom.

**Lamps add soft accent lighting.
A red shade matches the Fire
element, while a wooden stand
attracts more energy.**

The Water element

TRIGRAM: K'an
DIRECTION: north
COLOR: blue (black)
ASPIRATION: career prospects
SEASON: winter

The sight of the sea or the natural flowing water of a river or stream is relaxing and calming. Water is a strong natural force that at times can be turbulent, with rough, torrid currents, although generally it has the innate ability – like no other element – to pacify our stressed nerves and disturbed psyche. In feng shui, water is a positive symbol – an activator associated with the chill of winter and the colors blue and black – which is believed to attract wealth and prosperity. It is constantly moving around the home and environment carrying and accumulating positive chi.

Blue reflects the brightness of the sky and the stillness of a turquoise sea. Its coolness slows us down, making us unwind and take life at a more leisurely pace. Emotionally, it soothes and relieves tension, but on the negative side it can also fuel a depressed mind. When we look at this color, our heartbeat slows, our blood pressure drops, and we start to breathe more deeply.

Blue contains very yin (passive), soft energy, and can balance the excesses of Fire energy in the home. It has a calming presence when used in the north of your house. It relates to your Career sector – your achievement area, the place of future progression. Enhancing the northern sector of your house or a northern room can help to bring success in the workplace for all family members.

The serenity of blue

Blue is also about protection and comfort, and different hues of blue can enhance the peace of a north bedroom, since this is the place where we want to switch off from the world and sleep peacefully. As it is a slower, cooler color, blue particularly suits rooms in the north that have less movement. Aquamarine blues in a bathroom, for example, can encourage the process of letting go of stress and tension after a hard day's work. A living room can be a very social area, but

ts help to counteract
a bathroom's slow
atmosphere and
absorb humidity.

Wave shapes
visually boost
Water energy
and bring in
vitality.

Choosing a blue
you can live with
evokes feelings
of refreshment
and comfort.

Candles lift the
feeling of a
bathroom, as
yang Fire
energy balances
the room's yin
Water energy.

The dark blue tiles bring
in more water energy
than the walls.

also a place to sit and talk over the events of the day, so a light, soft blue creates a cool, airy space and induces feelings of calm.

Soft blues in a north-sited Water bathroom are very relaxing. The tiles here add some yang energy, balancing the yin cotton blind.

Energizing tones

A deep, dark-blue paint or wallpaper brings in the most Water energy, but sometimes this color can appear somber and heavy in room decoration, so look at all the different shades until you find one that inspires you every time you see it. There are numerous variations – bright blue, gray-blue, turquoise, or a soft light blue. Go through all the tones until you discover your favorite hue: the one that really works for you.

The yin and yang of Water

The tone of blue you choose for your north sector or room dictates how much of this less stimulating color you should introduce. It also indicates its strength – how yang (positive) it is, or how yin (passive). The deep midnight blue shade shown on this page is the strongest yang Water color, while the soft light blue is the most yin. In a

YANG BLUES

dining room, a strong yang blue creates an uplifting ambience, but you may prefer a soft yin blue in a bedroom to coax you to sleep. Soft blues still have a degree of stimulus, as they contain white, a Metal color which boosts the Water element.(Black is not considered here, as it is too heavy in decorating schemes, but can be used as an accent color.)

The different varieties of blue

A midnight blue or a lighter version gives you the purest Water energy in a room, but these shades may not appeal to or inspire you, so choose from other tones.

T i p

Painting the front door
The front door is the first impression people receive of your home, so it needs to look good and be kept in reasonable repair. To promote a positive flow of chi through a Water entrance, paint the door a deep blue, or to energize it further, decorate it white as Metal produces Water in the Element Cycle.

TURQUOISE
Refreshing, calm turquoise suits the slower ambience of a bathroom, but may feel too passive for a bustling family kitchen. It contains some green (Wood in the Element Cycle) which calms the Water energy. However, if turquoise is combined with electric blue kitchen units, the vibrations are lifted by this more fluorescent shade, making the energy more yang and positive.

YIN BLUES

LAVENDER BLUE
Lavender blue has a delicate and comforting vibration that can help boost confidence and self-esteem. It will nurture you in a bedroom, but may be too tranquil for a children's playroom. It contains some red, so the Fire energy takes away some of the Water vibrations.

STEEL BLUE
Steel blue can create a steadying, slightly formal atmosphere in a room. It is made up of blue, black, and white – the color of Metal which is the feeding energy of Water. It can help concentration in a home study, but may feel too austere in a dining room setting.

Think about the composition of your blue to gauge its effect. Pure midnight blue gives the strongest yang energy, while a soft blue brings in yin energy.

Colors to energize or calm Water

You may decide that your Water room, or northern section, needs more than strengthening energy, and requires some added stimulating color vibrations to make it a happy living space. Where there is continuous movement or animated social interaction, as in a hall, a kitchen, or a sociable dining room, it may be better to paint the area with its feeding color. For Water rooms, this is white, because Metal produces Water in the Element Cycle. Silver and gold also relate to the Metal element, so if you find a white room feels too stark and

The different Water colors and their actions

ROOM ELEMENT	COLOR	WHAT IT DOES
WATER	Blue (black)	Strengthens energy
Producing (feeding) *Element* Metal	White (metal and gold)	Energizes Water (good for rooms in which you are busy and creative)
Exhausting (calming) *Element* Wood	Green	Calms Water energy (good for rooms in which you relax)
Destroying *(controlling) Element* Earth	Yellow (beige)	Extinguishes Water energy
Clashing Element Fire	Red	Takes away Water energy

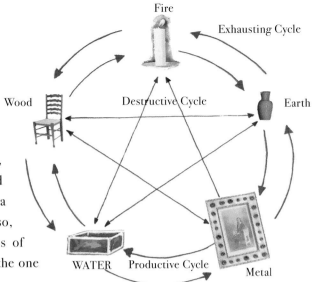

cold, you can add some warmth in a border, or stencil a frieze in these colors to add interest. You could also paint a chair rail or a picture rail using these metallic colors. Also, bear in mind that there are several tones of white that you can choose from, so select the one you like the best (see pages 130–131).

Sometimes a calming energy may be more appropriate to the room that you are decorating. We want some of our rooms to cosset us – after all, these are the places where we are trying to get rid of the worries of the working day. A shower room is such a sanctuary, a private place where we wash and soothe away all our cares and troubles. You can make this room more of a haven by painting it in a pleasant shade of green (see pages 110–111), because Wood calms Water in the Element Cycle.

White (Metal) boosts Water in the Productive Cycle, creating extra energy. For calm, add green (the Wood element). Keep Fire (red) and Earth (yellow and beige) colors to a minimum, as they clash with or destroy the Water element.

Conflicting colors

When you decorate your home with the Five Elements, there are colors that should only be used in small amounts in the different rooms, depending on their position.

In northern rooms, Water energy is destroyed by the element of Earth, so only include the colors yellow and beige sparingly in patterns or as spot color in wallpaper, soft furnishings, or rugs. And try not to feature checked, rectangular, or horizontal-striped patterns, or to crowd the room with ceramic ornaments. The other element that clashes with Water is Fire, so, again, bring only a little red in your scheme and avoid triangular, zigzag, and star patterns. Plan the room's lighting to be subtle, because, if there are too many bright lights, which represent the element of Fire, they can overwhelm the dominating Water energy.

Accessorizing a Water room

After selecting the blue for your north room or sector, you can buy accessories, fabrics, and furniture to enhance, calm, or energize your Water energy. If you have used an energizing white color, then add to this with some metal objects, or simply introduce some Water items. In a north room calmed with green, display some Wood ornaments (see page 94) and furniture or Water accessories.

How to energize

Displaying metallic items such as jewelry and scent bottles adds to the ambience of a Water room.

To increase the energy in a Water room, feature some metal or white accessories. Pictures of family or friends in silver, gold, or brass photograph frames can light up the east of any room, and emphasize the family energy already existing there. Metal side-tables and lamps with silvery bases increase sociability in living areas. The energy of a bathroom is always slow and languid, so hang a yang metal-framed mirror and use metal storage baskets, softening them with some yin, white fluffy towels and mats.

An iron bed brings Metal into a bedroom, but may be too energizing, and Metal also conducts electricity from power points and radiators. So lift the atmosphere of a bedroom by decorating it with different iron candlesticks. Decorative metal or white bowls can be placed on a dressing table overflowing with jewelry, toiletries, or cosmetics, while in a kitchen or dining room these bowls can hold fruit or snacks.

You can make the atmosphere more inviting in a hallway by placing a metal umbrella stand and clothes rack there, and displaying some inspiring pictures in metal frames.

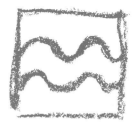

The shape of the Water element is wavy, which you can use in textiles and accessories to enhance the energy in a room.

Harmonizing your Water room

To enhance your newly decorated Water room, you can now go out and buy some blue or black accessories. Lamps, glazed dishes, small statues, aromatherapy burners, decorated boxes, plus some blue flowers or flowering plants will help to complete your room's decor (see also page 114). Bringing in hints of calming and stimulating energies creates yin and yang balance.

The shape that is associated with Water is irregular, so in a home decorating scheme you can bring cloud-like and wavy patterns into your wallpaper designs and furnishing fabrics.

Drapes and fabrics

To introduce the Water shape into your drapes, you can have a wavy or scalloped pelmet made or designed for you. Blend the shade of the drape material with your room's blue walls, and perhaps incorporate a soft cloud or muted pattern. By making the drapes a bit fuller, you will get them to hang in soft, flowing lines, emphasizing the Water movement. In a kitchen, a blue and white window blind will lift the room's energy slightly.

Accentuate and energize your Water room with blue and white, or gold and silver accessories, to represent the Water and Metal elements. Soft cushions are very yin and can balance yang materials such as glass or wood.

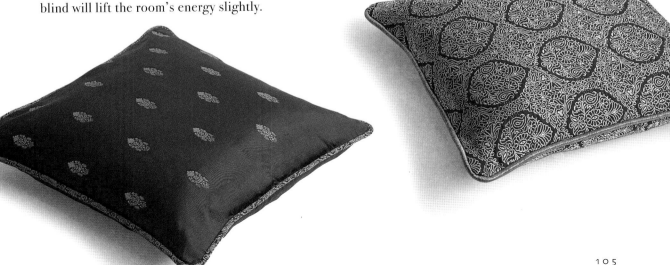

A classic reminder of the sky, clouds are one of the simplest Water motifs.

You can integrate the Water pattern into soft furnishings in a similar way. To balance energies, choose scatter cushions with stimulating white backgrounds and irregular patterns of calming green and neutral blue. If you always fall asleep on the sofa while watching television, select a stimulating white upholstery fabric to counteract this (Metal produces Water in the Element Cycle).

In the bathroom, you can have fun developing a seaside scheme by introducing a subtle wavy blue pattern on a white or clear plastic shower curtain. Turquoise or deep-blue thick towels and bathmats can suggest the color of the ocean, while a window blind with blue and white horizontal stripes is reminiscent of deckchair material.

The right furniture

As the Water shape is irregular, this gives you great scope to include wonderful fluid or organic lines in your living room furniture. These fresh, modern shapes also promote good conversation and sociability. Bold royal-blue or soft powder-blue fabrics can enrich pale-blue decorating schemes.

Fluid shapes for chairs, perhaps in blue plastic and metal, also suit an up-to-date dining room. The lack of square sides means that diners will not suffer any of the harsh, cutting chi that emanates from the corners or edges of more conventional chairs.

Wavy lines represent Water, and lend a fresh, modern sense to detail accessories, such as mugs, place mats, and plant pots.

Floor treatments

The color of the carpet can be a tone of white, green, or blue, but ideally make it a shade of blue to strengthen the Water energy emanating from the walls. If you have decorated a room using a mid-blue tone, then a slightly darker gray-blue or mauvish-blue carpet can contrast well. Natural wood flooring establishes clear, esthetic lines in the room, but will also slow down the energy in a Water room, as Wood calms Water in the Element Cycle.

There is scope in a Water area to use mottled, muted, or irregular patterns, often found in more modern styles of rugs. A large rug with a white background and a blue flowing design will create a dramatic impact in a hallway. Swirly patterns in blue, green, and white will also suit Water rooms. Only bring some specks of yellow, beige, or red into the patterns, because these colors are not harmonious with Water.

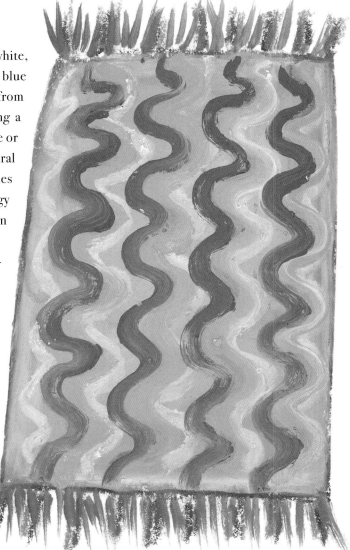

A blue rug with white and a wavy pattern emphasizes Water energy.

Water features

To promote more luck and good chi in your north living room, hall, or home study, you can keep some goldfish in an aquarium. Buy eight goldfish and one black (to absorb negativity), since the number nine is auspicious. Place it in the north sector (near the door) in your career corner, or in the southeast where it will help to improve your Wealth prospects. However, do not place an aquarium in a bedroom, kitchen, or bathroom, as water here can be too overwhelming.

Small fountain features can also be used in these areas, and the flowing, bubbling water is said to increase the flow of chi. An alternative way to enhance these corners is to fill a blue bowl with water and to light some floating candles in it – this provides excellent balance, with the yin of the blue and the yang of the burning candles.

An aquarium, ideally with nine fish, in a north room or area boosts prosperity.

The Wood element

TRIGRAM: Chen (east) Sun (southeast)
DIRECTION: east (strong Wood), southeast (small Wood)
COLOR: green
ASPIRATION: family and health (east), wealth and prosperity (southeast)
SEASON: spring
(Strong Wood has stronger energies than small Wood, so requires weaker shades of green)

Wood is an integral part of the natural world, representing new energy and springtime. When it is used in feng shui, Wood relates to green – a restful, calming, and balancing color that is neither hot nor cold. A great healer, particularly of the emotions of the heart, wood also soothes fears of being hurt or upset. The muddier tones are less positive and can promote boredom and inactivity. Physically it brings stability to blood circulation.

A compassionate, kind color that invites sharing, green is more yin and radiates passive energies that can particularly suit relaxation rooms. Green will bring equilibrium to two of the directions in your home – in the east, your Family and Health area, the place of good relationships with friends and family, of good health and vitality, of enthusiasm for life; and in the southeast, an influential part of the Pa Kua associated with Wealth and Prosperity. It represents the abundance that you have in your life, both materially and spiritually, your financial prospects, and future security.

A green, blue, and red rug is a perfect balance of all the energies.

For a living room in the east or southeast, rich greens provide a relaxing haven. A touch of Water (blue) adds stimulation, while Fire (red) energy is more calming.

Muslin drapes
emphasize the upright
Wood shape and bring
in a softer, yin green.

The red pattern on the
cushions brings in
some calming energy in
this relaxing room.

Candles represent
the Fire element.
They slow Wood
energy, creating a
peaceful tranquility.

Healthy green plants
with rounded leaves
reinforce Wood
energy and cleanse
the atmosphere.

The harmony of green

Green is a compassionate color that can prevent conflict, so a family breakfast room is good for one of its hues. It also promotes good decision-making, so, although it is a slower, more stable energy, it can help projects take shape in an eastern or southeastern study. Green inspires a great sense of space, so, in a conservatory, a light green creates airiness, reinforcing the room's connection with nature.

Stimulating shades

A stronger, natural green paint or wallpaper design will bring in the most vibrational energy to Wood rooms, but look at deep emerald, a mint green, or soft lime to find the tone that warms your heart.

The yin and yang of Wood

The type of green that you select for your east or southeast area or room will indicate how much energy of this less stimulating color you are bringing in. The color also relates to the strength of Wood energy – whether it is more yang (positive) or more yin (passive). Of the colors described on this page, moss green is the strongest yang Wood color, while soft mint green is the most yin color. A darker

YANG GREENS

shade of yang green is more stimulating for a child's busy playroom, while a soft, light yin green may be more to your taste in a Wood bathroom, where you soak away your troubles, hidden from the world. Soft green shades contain white, and are linked to Metal, which destroys Wood in the Element Cycle (see page 113), so be careful how much white is included in your chosen shade.

The different varieties of green

A moss green or a lighter shade of it brings strong Wood energies into a room, but these tones may not be to your taste, so make a selection from the other hues.

T'ip

Painting the front door

The entrance of your home says a lot about you, so keep the front door clear of vegetation and regularly clean it so it is free of cobwebs and dirt. To encourage good chi to come in through your Wood entrance, paint it a deep rich green. Water feeds Wood in the Element Cycle so, for more energy, use a strong blue to encourage the flow of energy around your home.

LIME GREEN

This is a fresh, lively color that reminds one of budding leaves. It can add vibrancy to kitchen units, but you may need a softer green on walls, as too much lime is overpowering. Avoid a very yellowy-lime, as it is unsettling. Yellow also relates to Earth, which clashes with Wood in the Element Cycle.

YIN GREENS

MINT GREEN

Mint green is a soft tone of green that is very restful to the eye. As it also contains a measure of blue, this color gives off some of the cooling, calming aspects of turquoise and blue (Water feeds Wood in the Element Cycle). This is a pleasing and restful color for a bedroom, but it may feel too slow and static for a regularly used dining area or room.

Moss green is very yang, giving strong Wood energy, while a soft pale green emits flower yin color vibrations.

OLIVE GREEN

This is a cooler shade of green with a slightly harder edge, as it has a touch of black in it, which also relates to the Water element (see above). Olive greens can suit the practical atmosphere of a utility or laundry room, but may be a bit harsh for a room used on a daily basis, particularly a convivial living area.

Colors to energize or calm Wood

Your Wood room or area will greatly benefit from the strengthening energy of its element color, green, but you may feel your room requires even higher color energy. Greater vibrancy can be especially useful in a kitchen, where people are constantly snacking, or coming and going, or in a study where the worker may feel the need for extra stimulation to produce innovative and creative ideas and to work more effectively. As the feeding element for Wood is Water, you can decorate these areas with blue, adding some touches of

The different Wood colors and their actions

ROOM ELEMENT	COLOR	WHAT IT DOES
WOOD	Green	Strengthens energy
Producing (feeding) Element Water	Blue (black)	Energizes Wood (good for rooms in which you are busy and creative)
Exhausting (calming) Element Fire	Red	Calms Wood energy (good for rooms in which you relax)
Destroying (controlling) Element Metal	White (metal and gold)	Extinguishes Wood energy
Clashing Element Earth	Yellow (beige)	Takes away Wood energy

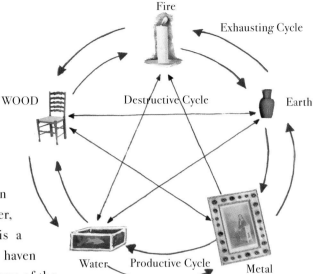

black as accent color on the woodwork if you prefer (see pages 100–101).

In other southern or southeastern rooms, you might wish to create a slower, more gentle atmosphere. A bedroom is a soothing place where we retreat; it is a haven where we rest our spirit and let our problems of the day drift away. Using a calm, soft shade of pink (Fire calms Wood in the Element Cycle) in this room will evoke wonderful feelings of peace and serenity.

Conflicting colors

Depending on a room's direction, the Element Cycle shows that some colors are not auspicious to use over large areas in certain rooms. In eastern and southeastern rooms, Wood energy will be destroyed by the Metal Element, so be sure to use white, silver, and gold sparingly in the decorating schemes and furnishings. It is also better not to feature too many ornaments or furniture with circular or oval patterns in these colors. The Earth Element also clashes with Wood, so if you want to use yellow or beige, limit it to a speck of color. Avoid displaying too many ceramic ornaments, or choosing square, rectangular, or horizontal patterns for the curtains or other furnishings.

Still, conflicting energies can be used to advantage. If you are a particularly argumentative person who often flares up when people visit, try this experiment. Place a white cover on the sofa you normally sit on in your Wood lounge, or include some white cushions there. This takes away some of the energy from that area which may help to make you less fiery. You can occasionally use conflicting energies for your personal improvement.

Maximize your Wood room with the element colors, Wood green and Water blue, which feed Wood in the Element Cycle. Earth (yellow) and Metal (white) colors cause clashing energies, so it is usually best to minimize these in a Wood room.

Accessorizing a Wood room

When you have found the right shade of green for your east or south-east room or area, you can start considering the accessories, soft furnishings, and furniture that will strengthen, calm, or stimulate your Wood energy. With an energized room, bring in blue or black objects or wooden items. Alternatively, if the energy is calmed with red, add Fire (see page 124) or Wood accessories.

Vases in wavy shapes in blacks and blues show the Water element, which boosts Wood energy.

How to energize

To boost your Wood room, introduce some Water or blue and black accessories. Royal-blue glass or ceramic bowls, piled high with fruit, nuts, or savory snacks, have a luminous quality, creating a feeling of abundance, as well as lifting the energy in living areas. Blue- or black-patterned, modern, wavy vases can form focal points on any table. Filling them with delicate blue flowers will emphasize their vibrancy in a Wood room.

Working from home is often intense, so give yourself some more energy around your desk by getting a computer with a blue casing, a matching printer, and desk lamp. For an extra boost, buy some blue files and stationery holders, and watch your work output start to increase.

Aquariums or small fountains (see page 107) are auspicious water features that increase the flow of chi. In a Wood living room, they promote wealth prospects in the southeast and good family health in the east. Although moving water is best, a simple glass vase or dish filled with pebbles and water is still a very effective feature.

Harmonizing your Wood room

Now that you have finished the decoration of your Wood room, you can balance its energies by sourcing some wooden or green accessories. Carved wooden bowls, boxes, or ethnic masks, houseplants, green glasses, bottles, lampshades, and other items will finish your interior scheme (see also page 94). Introducing accents of calming and stimulating energies brings yin and yang balance.

With the Element system, each element relates to a shape. In the case of Wood, this is upright. So, for the home, look for wallpaper designs or soft furnishings that have vertical, striped patterns.

Avoid green overkill by balancing Wood colors with natural, rough-hewn wooden accessories such as these hand-made pots. Bear in mind that the use of the element itself, as well as its color, will add postive elemental energy.

Drapes and fabrics

To reinforce the upright Wood symbol in your style of drapes, hang them from a wooden pole, keeping them long, and judge the fullness carefully so that they create a tall, rectangular shape. Make the color of your drapes either a muted or stronger shade of the green that is featured on the walls. A subtle, vertical striped pattern in the fabric will increase the Wood energy here.

The Wood pattern can also be integrated into all your soft furnishings. However, if you want your lounge to be one of your most relaxed areas, choose a soft red or pink fabric for your sofas and chairs, because Fire calms Wood in the Element Cycle. If you simply want to bring in a little calming energy, choose a deep-moss or emerald-green suite, but try to find a fabric that has a red pattern

Stars and zigzag patterns are linked to the Fire element and harmonize with Wood rooms.

(ideally a zigzag or star design). However, if you have one chair where you like to feel a bit more vibrancy – because here you read stimulating novels, look through your correspondence, do some light work, or generally need to be able to concentrate – add some bright-blue cushions in order to give you this extra energy. Bright blues work here because Water produces or gives energy to Wood in the Element Cycle.

Soft sage or light apple-greens on your bedding will bring in a gentle Wood energy. If you feel that you need to introduce more color, then try muted patterns of red and blue, which will harmonize the calming and feeding elements. It is best not to have a white bottom sheet or white pillowcases, as Metal is the destroying energy of Wood.

The right furniture

Sofas and chairs with higher, more upright backs will help to give emphasis to the Wood shape in a living area. In a dining area, as already mentioned (see page 94), a round or an oval table is auspicious for all the diners and supports the Wood energy.

Water is the harmonizing energy for Wood, so choose accessories for your Wood room with wavy patterns and strong blues.

However, you can vary the type of energy that you introduce through your choice of wood. A table in a living or dining room made of softwood, such as pine or beech, will bring in more yin, passive energy, while the dark hardwoods, such as oak or teak, will bring in more active, yang energy. A wooden bed will embrace you when

placed in a Wood bedroom, and including a high, upright, solid headboard and footboard will enhance the Wood shape, giving you the protection you need when you are at your most vulnerable and fast asleep. Do remember that softer, rounded corners are good for bedroom furniture, particularly for your bed headboard and footboard, because this minimizes negative, cutting energy created by sharp corners and edges that can disturb you as you slumber.

Verdant green throws in rich fabrics add Wood energy to sofas, or create a stable, grounding ambience if used on a bed.

Floor treatments

If you are in a position to purchase a new carpet, you can make a choice from shades of blue, red, or green, but it is better to use green, as it enhances the presence of the Wood element. If you have used a sea-green wallpaper, for example, then a lighter, soft shade on the carpet will provide balance and be more restful on the eye. Natural wood flooring is perfect to use in a Wood room, and it does not slow the flow of chi energy in the same way as carpet (which is more yin). Every type of wood has a special warmth and uniqueness that makes it immensely appealing.

Rugs can make a stunning impact on flooring or neutral carpets. Look out for one with vertical stripes that will link it to the Wood shape. If the design can introduce the other elements, with the colors blue and red as well as green, it will harmonize all the energies. Avoid a white background or too much yellow, because these are the colors that do not work well with Wood. Floral patterns will encourage Wood's natural affinity with nature.

The Earth  element

Trigram: Ken (northeast), K'un (southwest)
Direction: northeast (small Earth),
southwest (strong Earth)
Color: yellow, beige
Aspiration: education and knowledge
(northeast), marriage and romantic
happiness (southwest)
Season: late summer
*(Strong Earth has stronger energies than
small Earth, so requires weaker shades
of yellow)*

Earth is everywhere in nature – in fields, pastures, gardens; it is also the soil beneath our feet. Heavy and solid, it seems dependable, and is associated with the long days of late summer, with plants and crops ready for harvest. In feng shui, the element of Earth is associated with yellow and beige. Cheerful and enriching, yellow is the color of the hot sun, and has the capacity to raise our spirits and stimulate the intellect. Negatively, it can induce egotistical feelings or sensations of irritability and occasionally nausea. It can also slightly raise blood pressure.

Glowing, radiant yellow is very yang (positive), and is suited to busy, active rooms. It harmonizes the energies in the northeast, your Education and Knowledge corner – a place of learning and career achievement; and in the southwest, your area of Marriage and Romantic happiness. By enhancing these sectors, you are promoting career success, and encouraging new and happy, loving relationships.

The red on the kitchen counter brings in more Fire energy. Keep the surface uncluttered for good chi flow.

Strong, warm yellows embrace an earth kitchen in the northeast or southwest. The red flooring and work-top here bring in some necessary stimulation.

A paler yellow for cabinet units includes some white, representing the Metal element that feeds Earth.

Rich, powerful yellow on the walls is blended with softer shades on the cabinets for harmony and balance.

A terra-cotta floor brings in some feeding Fire energy, ideal in this busy room.

The vitality of yellow

Yellow has powerful vibrations that can energize a sleepy brain, so in a northeast or southwest bathroom, a subtle yellow can bring you from a half-asleep state into positive action or work mode. In a playroom, these vibrant hues provide good mental stimulation for children, and, in a study, yellow creates confidence and focuses the mind on the tasks or projects of the day ahead.

Energizing hues

The stronger and richer the yellow you choose, the more Earth vibrations you will bring into a room. From buttercup yellow to pale lemon or a warm sand – find the shade that will fill you with delight every time you look at it.

The yin and yang of Earth

The hue of the yellow that you want to use in your northeast or southwest area or room dictates the energy levels of the stimulating color that you are introducing. Your chosen shade also shows the strength of the Earth energy, whether it is more yang (positive) or more yin (passive). Of the colors described on this page, golden yellow is the strongest Earth color, while soft beige-yellow is the

YANG YELLOWS

most yin color. A bright, yang yellow in an Earth breakfast room can make everyone who eats there feel uplifted and inspired, while a creamy, light yellow can be more relaxing in a tranquil bedroom. The lighter yellows, such as cream, bring in some white, adding some calming energy, because Metal calms Earth in the Element Cycle (see page 123).

The different varieties of yellow

A rich, golden yellow or a lighter shade allows the stronger energies of the Earth element to come into a room, but if these are not the tones for you, find another hue that is more to your liking.

Painting the front door
Your front door can say a lot about you and how you live. To keep positive chi flowing in through your Earth entrance, keep the area clean and tidy. Paint the door as strong a yellow as you can bear; for even more energy, paint it a bright red, because Fire produces Earth in the Element Cycle. Light the doorway and, if you feel in need of some protection, place a pair of Fu dogs outside on either side of the door.

LEMON YELLOW
This is a slightly cooler shade, but one that has a fresh, vital appeal. It will embrace a sunny southwest dining room that is used for long, Mediterranean-style summer lunches. The color contains a fair bit of white, which gives some calming energy, because Metal calms Earth in the Element Cycle.

YIN YELLOWS

ZINGY YELLOW
Zingy yellow describes a vibrant hue that is ideal in busy, lively rooms. As it can be quite overpowering in large expanses, try painting some on the cabinets in a kitchen , for example, and then using a softer, less strident yellow on the walls. This helps balance a strong yellow without missing out on its zingy impact. The warm, uplifting vibrations of these two colors together will make this a happy and fun room for all.

SAFFRON YELLOW
This is a delightful color. It has the warmth of yellow with a hint of the fire of orange (Fire feeds Earth in the Element Cycle). It is a distinctive, yet deceptively easy shade to live with. In a lounge, for example, it can help engender congeniality and sparkling, enthralling conversation.

A strong canary yellow brings in the most yang energy, while a soft, creamy shade introduces yin energy.

Colors to energize or calm Earth

Strengthening the energies of your Earth room or area with yellow or beige will make it a much more pleasant place to be, but often you may feel that more energy is necessary in this particular space to produce the right atmosphere. In a family hallway, where there is a constant buzz as your children and their friends come and go, you can feed in more energy by decorating it in a shade of red, because Fire produces Earth in the Element Cycle.

In other northeast or southwest rooms, a more restful energy may be more appropriate to help you achieve a mellow mood. If you have

The Different Earth colors and their actions

ROOM ELEMENT	COLOR	WHAT IT DOES
EARTH	Yellow (beige)	Strengthens energy
Producing (feeding) Element Fire	Red	Energizes Earth (good for rooms in which you are busy and creative)
Exhausting (calming) Element Metal	White (metal, gold)	Calms Earth energy (good for rooms in which you relax)
Destroying (controlling) Element Wood	Green	Extinguishes Earth energy
Clashing Element Water	Blue (black)	Takes away Earth energy

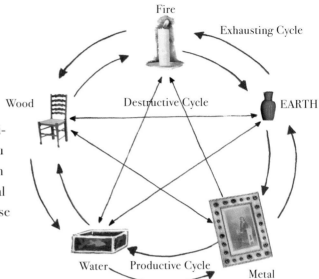

your own special room – a relaxation or meditation room that you love – a space where you allow some time each day just for you, then painting it in a tone of white (because Metal calms Earth in the Element Cycle) will increase the peaceful vibrations that you feel there.

Conflicting colors

When you practice the Five Element system, you will find that there are also colors that are best avoided, or used minimally, in different rooms, depending on their orientation. In northeast and southwest rooms, the Earth energy is destroyed by the Wood element, so when you plan your design scheme, only feature green in spot color in your wallpaper designs or soft furnishings. And try to limit the amount of wooden furniture and ornaments that you have in the room, remembering that vertical striped patterns in your furnishings also destroy Earth energy.

The other element that works against, or clashes with, Earth is Water, which is associated with blue and black, so only include accents of this color (if at all) in your room. Also, control the amount of blue accessories here and do not display water features, such as aquariums or small fountains, because they accentuate the presence of the draining Water energy. When selecting soft furnishings, such as drape, cushion, or rug designs, steer away from any with cloudlike or wavy patterns.

Sometimes the colors of conflicting energies can help in a particular situation. If you have a difficult relative living with you, who upsets everyone in the household, try covering his or her favorite chair with some green fabric, which is the controlling energy of Earth, and see if their mood improves.

Fire (red) feeds Earth in the Element Cycle, adding more energy to an Earth room, while Metal brings in some calming energy. Water (blue and black) and Wood (green) colors, however, deplete Earth energy, so use them sparingly, if at all.

Accessorizing
an Earth room

Candles are wonderful in an Earth room, as Fire yang energy boosts Earth and adds a special ambience.

Once you have found the yellow shade for your northeast or southwest room or area, you can think about the accessories, furniture, and fabrics that will harmonize, calm, or stimulate the existing Earth energy. Where you have energized rooms with the feeding color of red, add some red ornaments, lights, and candles, or use some Earth items. In rooms calmed with white, bring in some Metal (see page 104–107) or Earth accessories.

How to energize

To stimulate your Earth room, buy some red or Fire accessories. A red or pink lamp, vase, or bowl, several large candles, or a row of tea lights in a stone block can ignite the atmosphere in living areas. Place some of them in the south of the room, so that your Recognitionand Fame area receives the benefit of these uplifting vibrations.

Bring a burst of fiery vitality to the slightly stagnant energy of the bathroom by having an orange window blind, fluffy burnt-orange towels, and bathmat there. Lit candles in sconces on the wall will reflect the orange hues, giving out large pools of warm, inviting light when you're bathing.

Red elements, such as a trash can, canisters, kettle, cups, and kitchen utensils can all enliven the energy of a kitchen. They also look striking against warm yellow walls.

The shape of the Earth element is the square or rectangle. You can incorporate it in accessories to maximize a room's energy.

Harmonizing your Earth room

To balance the energies in your Earth room, once it is decorated, you can add some yellow or ceramic accessories – woven yellow storage baskets, yellow frosted bowls, vases, or glasses, Oriental stone statues, ceramic planters, a selection of large and small pebbles, yellow flowers, or flowering plants – to help achieve the look you are seeking (see also page 134). Incorporating some touches of the calming and stimulating energies allows for yin and yang balance.

Each of the Five Elements has its own shape, and in the case of Earth this is a square or rectangle. So, when you want to enhance the Earth energies in your home, look for wallpaper designs or fabrics with checked or subtle horizontal stripe patterns.

Drapes and fabrics

You can use the Earth shape in your drapes by having a rectangular pelmet made. Choose a coordinating drape material so that it is slightly stronger or lighter than the color on your walls. Letting the drapes hang in long, straight lines (not too full) will strengthen the Earth shape, and featuring a delicate checked pattern in the weave will further emphasize it.

Look for square or rectangle designs in textiles in yellow or beige Earth colors. This brings together solidity and vibrancy, two strong Earth qualities.

Think of other ways that you can use the Earth pattern in your furnishing materials. When you are deciding on which seating fabrics you can bring into a room, beige-yellow cotton or linen materials on sofas and chairs can be better in the long term than more vibrant shades, of which you may soon tire. Scatter a mixture of ocher and cream linen or silk cushions on the seating to provide some calming energy. Buy a few red cushions if there is one seating area you feel is in need of extra stimulus, to give you more concentration for reading. White throws or blankets have a relaxing effect on the people who are sitting on them, and they also make a stunning contrast to yellow sofas.

The Earth element is linked to ceramics and many of these can have an aged, rustic quality. On simple shapes, this can create a more modern look.

Yellow can be a difficult color to live with in a bedroom, so, in order to induce sound sleep, search out the softer shades for all your bedding. Too strong a yellow will usually feel overstimulating, and it may cause restlessness or insomnia. White pillows and sheets will help slow down the energy and encourage soothing sleep rhythms.

The right furniture

Pale-yellow sofas and chairs with square backs and arms will reinforce the Earth shape in your lounge. For dining, choose a round or rectangular glass table with an iron frame, so that you achieve an equal balance of both neutral and calming

Rectangular shapes, singly or as part of a striped design, stand for the Earth element.

energies. High-backed chairs covered in yellow suede-like fabrics will add colorful interest, give support when eating, and ensure spontaneous conversation. Try to keep the number of chairs even; six or eight chairs, for instance, is considered to be auspicious. A wooden table is not a feasible option in an Earth dining area, because the Wood element destroys this energy.

In a kitchen, stimulating red stools around a yellow breakfast bar will help to give people a healthy appetite and promote a good start to every working day.

Floor treatments

You can add energizing red or pink or calming cream with your choice of carpet, but a shade of yellow will build on the color vibrations you have used on the walls. With a colorwashed yellow, a fudgey-beige carpet can blend well. Wood flooring, although normally a favored choice, is best avoided in an Earth room because it destroys the beneficial energies there.

Long runners can make a striking impact in halls, particularly in large houses. A brown-orange background brings in some feeding energy, while horizontal white stripes enhance the Earth shape and impart a touch of calm. Modern, square patterns with red, yellow, and white balance all the energies, but choose designs with only a little green, blue, or black, because these colors disrupt the area's Earth energies. Placing soft yellow or cream plain cotton rugs (which are more yin in nature) in bathrooms can balance the coldness and yang energy of ceramic tiles.

Stone, ceramic, and terra-cotta tiles are part of the Earth element and are highly durable in kitchens, bathrooms, and hallways. You can also use red quarry tiles, which are easy to maintain, to bring in some feeding energy.

The Metal element

Metal has a solid, supportive strength – a grounding presence that evokes safe feelings of consistency and reliability. In the practice of feng shui, it is associated with the energy of money, cashflow, and what we can achieve through our own efforts. Metal also represents late fall, a golden time when the fruits of the harvest are gathered in and the growing season is nearing completion. It symbolizes the deep glow of the sun as it sets in the west.

TRIGRAM: Tui (west), Ch'ien (northwest)
DIRECTION: west (small Metal), northwest (strong Metal)
ASPIRATION: children (west), mentors, and networking (northwest)
SEASON: fall
(Strong Metal has stronger energies than small Metal, so requires weaker shades of white)

The main color of Metal is white, a pure protective color that can give us space in which to grow and develop in our lives. It can bring about an inner cleansing of the mind, emotions, and spirit, and can help to alleviate shock or despair. Physically, white is a color that can give our bodies more energy. It is a positive, yang, stimulating hue, but too much pure white in the home can induce feelings of isolation and hinder decision-making.

White balances the energy in two parts of your home. One is the west, your Children area, a place of new beginnings that represents your hopes for the future, and fertility. The northwest is your Mentors and Networking area, the space of useful contacts and good prospects, of strength and leadership. By enhancing the chi in these Metal corners, you are increasing your opportunities in new areas, boosting the luck of your offspring, and enticing helpful people into your own or your family's life.

The freedom of white

White increases the feeling of space within a room, giving it an inviting, airy appeal, and a warmer white will expand a narrow hall, inspiring optimism in all who enter your home. It is also a spiritual color, so a white tone will add some pure light to a tiny bathroom, encouraging family members to relax more deeply and reflect on their lives while bathing.

A gold stencil adds energy to the white walls.

A metal mirror strengthens the energy here and helps increase the space in a hallway.

A metal light fitting boosts Metal energy. Good lighting makes a hall more inviting.

Yellow flooring brings in stimulating Earth energy, and is ideal for an entrance.

A violet-white shade on the walls softens the overall effect.

Stimulating tones

A strong white paint with a hint of another color, or a white wallpaper with a silver or gold pattern, will attract more energy vibrations to your Metal rooms, but look at all the hues until you find the one that most attracts you. White is a difficult color to use in the home, as there are not so many variations, but go through the different shades – blue-whites, pink-whites, and beige-whites – until you find the one that is right for you.

A soft shade of white is best for a hallway in the west or northwest. The warmer yellow on the floor adds stimulating energy to welcome guests.

The yin and yang of Metal

The shade of white favored for your west or northwest area
or room reflects the level of energy of this stimulating color.
Your chosen color also shows the strength of this energy – whether
it is more yang (positive) or more yin (passive). As noted previously,
white does not have the depth of variation of the other elemental
colors, but you can still find your own special shade by

YANG

looking at the subtle tonal differences available.
Violet-white above is the strongest yang Metal
color, while a soft white is the most yin color.
Silver and gold bring in more yang Metal
energy, but use them only in small amounts
in a room. A darker blue-white can open up a
rather depressing, small-Metal utility or laundry room, harmonizing its overall energy. The
slight coldness of the color is unlikely to affect
family members, because this is a room that is
not regularly visited. A warmer, more yin white with
a touch of yellow can embrace you in a dressing room,
where you deliberate on your clothes for the day ahead.
The presence of yellow brings in some stimulation, because
Earth feeds Metal in the Element Cycle (see page 133).

T͜ip

Painting the front door

Your front door is your eye on the world, and also where visitors first enter, so keep the paintwork well maintained. Flowering tubs on each side of the door will invite people to enter and encourage good chi flow. To strengthen your Metal entrance, paint it a strong shade of white; for extra energy, decorate it in yellow, because Earth produces Metal in the Element Cycle.

Whites, plus silver and gold

White is a neutral hue, and in large areas this Metal color may feel too isolating and in need of a little uplifting color from its calming and energizing elements (blue and yellow). However, there are whites within the yin and yang color range that you may prefer to the strongest Metal color (violet-white).

YIN

Violet-white is the purest and most yang Metal color, while soft white is the most yin, and emits a more gentle energy. Strong metallic colors are yang and work well as decorative details.

ROSE-WHITE

This has a warmer vibrancy because it brings just a hint of red. It can lift the atmosphere in a small kitchen.

VIOLET-WHITE

This also has some red warmth, but also energizing, cooler blue. It introduces a stimulating, but contemplative, ambience to a study.

SILVER

A silver chair rail, picture rail, or border in a white room strengthens existing Metal energy; the moon's color, it radiates feminine vibrations.

GOLD

This relates to the sun and abundance. As an accent color, it can inspire and revitalize. Shades of gold on woodwork can look striking.

Colors to energize or calm Metal

Harmonizing your Metal room or area with white will dramatically improve the atmosphere, but you may feel that you need some extra stimulation here. If you regularly entertain friends and family and want a Metal dining room that promotes conviviality and witty conversation over long meals far into the night, then decorating it with its feeding color will give extra animation to the room's atmosphere. With Metal this color is yellow or beige (see pages 00–00), because Earth produces Metal in the element cycle.

Complementary Metal colors and their actions

ROOM ELEMENT	COLOR	WHAT IT DOES
Metal	White (metal, gold)	Strengthens energy
Producing (feeding) Element Earth	Yellow (beige)	Energizes Metal (good for rooms in which you are busy and creative)
Exhausting (calming) Element Water	Blue (black)	Calms Metal energy (good for rooms in which you relax)
Destroying (controlling) Element Fire	Red	Extinguishes Metal energy
Clashing Element Wood	Green	Takes away Metal energy

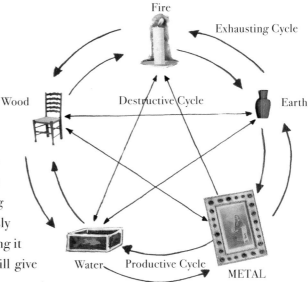

In other west or northwest rooms you may desire a more enveloping, peaceful energy. Water calms Metal in the element cycle, so if you love spending time alone in your bathroom, soaking luxuriously in the bath surrounded by candles, then decorating it in calming shades of blue (see pages 00–00) will give your more blissful moments here.

Conflicting colors

Due to the way the Five Element system works, there will also be colors that are best featured only as spot colors in different rooms, depending on their compass direction. In the case of Metal, the Fire element destroys it, so only include a little red in wallpaper designs, soft furnishings, or floor treatments in your room. And restrict the amount of red accessories and candles that you display, keep lighting subdued, and try not to feature strong zigzag, star, or triangular patterns on sofas, drapes, or cushions.

The Wood element, which is associated with green, also clashes with Metal, so bring in this color discreetly in patterns in a Metal room. Vertical, striped materials also enhance the Wood element, so they are best excluded from your overall design. Feature only a little wooden furniture and ornaments in your scheme, because once again they enhance the presence of the Wood element.

Sometimes it can be appropriate to use a conflicting energy to resolve a problem in the home. If you have a young baby who is constantly crying and has problems sleeping through the night, it is worth experimenting with the destroying element in their cot. With a Metal room this is red, so try a pink cot quilt and see if the sleep patterns improve.

Use Earth colors to energize your Metal room or area, along with the whites, silvers and golds of the Metal element itself. Keep Fire and Wood colors at bay, as they undermine Metal.

Accessorizing a Metal room

Choosing the right tone of white for your west or northwest room or sector can take some time, but, once you have decided on it, you can start having fun choosing the accessories, furniture, and fabrics that will emphasize, calm, or increase its Metal energy. For rooms you have energized with yellow or beige on the walls, introduce some yellow or ceramic objects or Metal ornaments. Alternatively, with a Metal room with calming blue energy, fill it with Water (see page 104) or Metal accessories.

White represents Metal, and the circular shape of the cushion also reinforces Metal energy.

How to energize a Metal room

To lift the energy levels in your Metal room, display some yellow and ceramic accessories. Large Grecian-style earthenware or terra-cotta pots that sit on the floor bring in a wonderful Earthy energy to living areas. When full of yellow silk flowers and placed in the northeast of the room, they can encourage growth in your Education and Knowledge area. In your southwest (Marriage and Romantic Happiness) corner, you can attract a new partner, or foster extra feelings of love in an existing relationship, with ceramic statues of romantically entwined couples or paired stone items, such as hearts, ducks, or doves.

A yellow pottery teapot and breakfast set brings in earthy warm energy to a cool white kitchen, while, in a creamy bathroom, yellow ceramic soap dishes, toothbrush holders, and candle holders add a ray of sunshine.

Harmonizing your Metal room

To balance the energies in your Metal room, once you have finished decorating, you can start to search for white or metal (gold or silver) accessories. Iron candlesticks, metal-framed mirrors, metal clocks, gold or aluminum light fittings, lamps, steel planters, white bowls, dishes, candles, vases, and fresh white flowers will make the room feel complete (see also page 104). Including some of the colors of the calming and stimulating energies gives you yin and yang balance.

All of the Five Elements also have a relevant shape, and, in the case of Metal, it is a dome or circular shape. To use this in your home decorating scheme, choose oval or circular patterns for your soft furnishings or wallpapers.

Brushed silver accessories bring style to a modern Metal room. Search for vases cast in unusual circle shapes to enhance your room's energy.

Drapes and fabrics

You can bring the Metal shape into the design of your drapes by having a domed or semicircular pelmet above them or, if you prefer, featuring soft rolls of fabric that drape over the pelmet will enhance it. Match the drape color to the shade of white on the walls, maybe considering a stronger tone in a cotton or muslin fabric with a subdued circular pattern. If you feel that the room is starting to look too neutral, add cream curtains, but include some calming blue and feeding yellow energy in a pattern on them.

Introduce the Metal pattern in the same way in the rest of your soft furnishings. If you love the style of cream sofas in cotton, wool, or soft leather, but are worried about their practicality on a day-to-day basis, then cream fake-fur throws will keep them looking new –

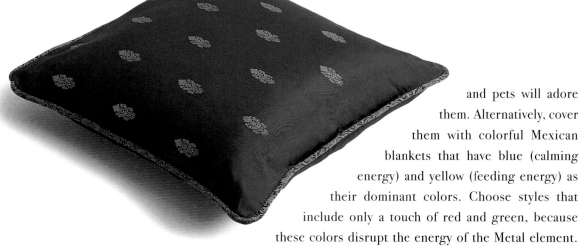

Blue cushions are an easy accessory for Metal rooms, as the blues symbolize the Water element, which supports Metal.

and pets will adore them. Alternatively, cover them with colorful Mexican blankets that have blue (calming energy) and yellow (feeding energy) as their dominant colors. Choose styles that include only a touch of red and green, because these colors disrupt the energy of the Metal element. Blue cushions in tactile suede or silky materials will make sofas and chairs more relaxing.

In a bedroom, crisp white cotton or linen bedding is fresh and appealing; creamier colors add a bit of stimulation. If you are a restless sleeper, place a deep-blue bedspread on the bed to surround you with an aura of calm.

The right furniture

White sofas with long, rounded backs and chairs with semicircular backs (all with rounded arms) are yin and will support the Metal shape. As Wood clashes with Metal, look for an iron dining table with a round or rectangular glass top. It will look modern and stylish, and glass makes an ideal surface for inspired dining, because it is part of the Earth element, which feeds Metal in the Element

Oval or circular patterns are present in both modern graphics and ancient symbols. Use them to strengthen your room's Metal energy.

Cycle. In living areas, small side-tables with tiled tops and iron legs add balance and harmony.

As mentioned in the Water section (see page 104), in feng shui iron beds are not ideal in bedrooms, so choose a wooden bed. However, since this is a clashing element, boost the Metal presence with a white mattress and bedding.

White bedlinen boosts Metal energy, counteracting the presence of the Wood energy of the bed frame, which is more draining.

Floor treatments

A creamy carpet looks stunning, but a beige shade with some stimulating Earth energy, or a blue tone with some calming Water energy, may need less cleaning and wear better. Wooden flooring is not a good idea in Metal rooms, as it works against the element.

Modern, circular white rugs with bold, flowing, rounded blue and yellow patterns can form the focal point in a living area or hall. Pretty floral designs with some green and red also promote a circular shape.

In kitchens and hallways, where the flooring is in constant use, ceramic floor tiles can be very hardwearing. They are part of the Earth element, which energizes Metal, so use tones of beige or yellow. White and some calming black tiles in a kitchen give a clean, streamlined appearance. Marble tiles, flecked with black, will have the same effect. And slate is a wonderful stone, with variegated patterns of blues and grays, and will bring a bit of slower energy into the kitchen area.

Color Chart

This color chart is included to show you that when you are painting your rooms according to their elements (see pages 88–137) there is a variety of color families that you can use within each major color. So for example if you are not very keen on classic red but you have some Fire rooms, you can

MAUVEY REDS (FIRE ROOMS)

YANG   YIN

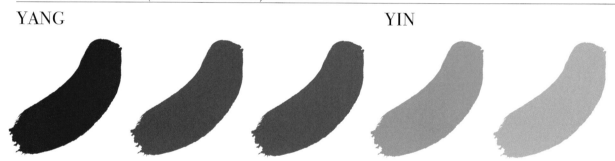

A balancing color family not as stimulating as the pure reds as they contain blue, Water, which destroys some of the Fire energy. Choose a shade that appeals from the yang–yin range.

STEELY BLUES (WATER ROOMS)

YANG   YIN

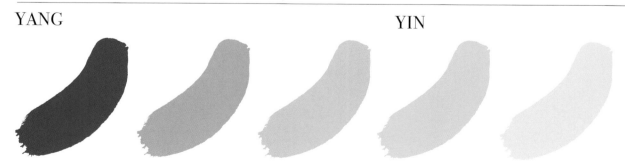

A slightly formal color family that contains some white, Metal, the feeding color of Water. Choose the shade for you from the yang–yin range.

have a look at the shades on page 90–91 or decide
that a yang or yin shade of mauvey-red or orangey-
red suits you better. There is not room to include
all the color families here, but you can easily
obtain different color swatches from your local
DIY stores or specialist paint shops.

PINK REDS (FIRE ROOMS)

YANG   YIN

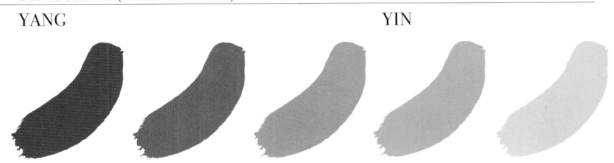

A softer family of reds that are not as fiery as true reds. They also contain some white,
Metal, a clashing element. Choose your favorite shade from the yang–yin range.

TURQUOISE BLUES (WATER ROOMS)

YANG   YIN

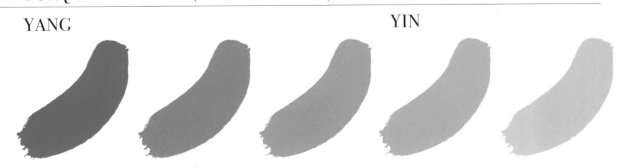

A refreshing but more passive color family that contains some green, Wood, which calms
the Water energy. Choose the shade that appeals from the yang–yin range.

OLIVE GREENS (WOOD ROOMS)

YANG   YIN

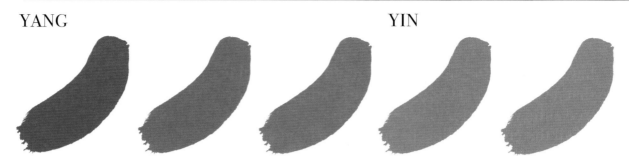

A cooler color family with a slightly harder edge. It contains some black, Water, which calms the Wood vibrations. Choose your best shade from the yang–yin range.

ZINGY YELLOWS (EARTH ROOMS)

YANG   YIN

A warm and uplifting color family, but take care about painting the yang hues over large expanses as they can be too much. Choose the shade in the yang–yin range that you love.

ORANGEY REDS (FIRE ROOMS)

YANG   YIN

A color family that carries less heat than pure red. It is a creative color with some yellow, Earth, calming energy. Choose the shade you like from the yang-yin range.

LIME GREENS (WOOD ROOMS)

YANG   YIN

A vibrant color family that adds a fresh appeal to rooms, but beware of including shades with too much yellow, Earth, as this clashes with Wood. Choose the shade in the yang-yin range that stands out for you.

SAFFRON YELLOWS (EARTH ROOMS)

YANG   YIN

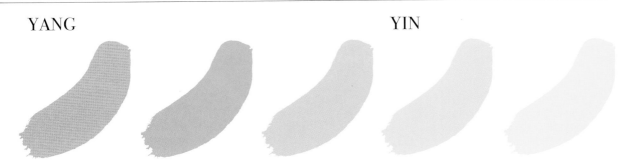

A delightful warm color family that contains some of the zest of orange. Choose the shade that draws you in from the yang–yin range.

MAROON REDS (FIRE ROOMS)

YANG   YIN

This deeper red family has a strong warmth, but does contain some black, Water, which takes away some of the Fire energy. Choose your shade from the yang-yin range.

Using the Color Compass

You can use your color compass to map out the aspirational areas of your home (see page 87), to map out each room individually, or to check what colors to paint different rooms or areas once you know the directional element.

To map out your home, draw a plan of it to scale on graph paper, then from corner to corner draw two diagonal lines that meet in the center. If you have a missing section, draw it in as illustrated below. You can physically add mirrors to a wall that borders a missing section – here, a mirror should be hung in the hall, so the missing section is symbolically filled in.

Next, add in the directions of your home, based on the reading taken from the front door (see page 86).

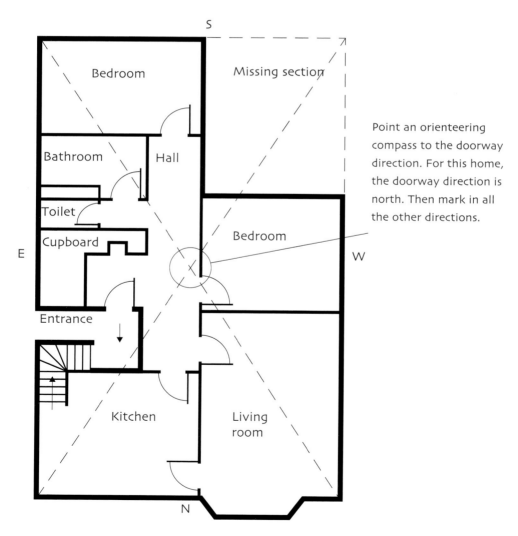

Point an orienteering compass to the doorway direction. For this home, the doorway direction is north. Then mark in all the other directions.

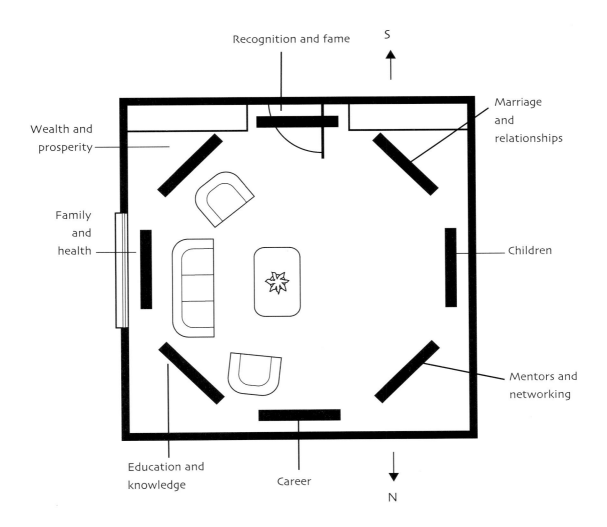

Place your color compass over your room, or area, matching it to the door direction and mark off your aspirational areas as shown. Look at the room's colors – for example, the room above is a Fire room, so it needs to be a shade of red. Look at some of the yang or yin shades you can choose (see pp 138-41). If you want to map out room by room so that you can find out the individual elements and aspirational areas, work as above but make a separate plan for each room. Just check the directions, and then lay the color compass over the plan to locate your aspirational areas.

Using crystals

Crystals are great energizers and can help to lift the vibrations of your different aspirational areas. You can use rose quartz (a love crystal) in your Marriage and Relationships area in the southwest, and a natural quartz in your Education and Knowledge area in the northeast. A tiger's eye helps with your business dealings, so place it in your Career space in the north.

The Color Compass

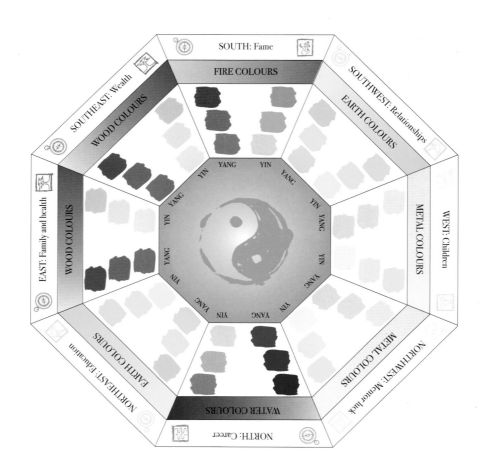